PRAISE FOR *COURSE DESIGN FORMULA*®

"If you plan to start an online course or if you simply want to improve your online teaching skills, take the time to read *Course Design Formula*. How do students actually learn? What affordances and constraints are directly associated with online teaching? The author bases her book on simple psychology and pedagogy principles, cognitive science research, as well as her rich experience as an educator, both online and offline. Even at 400 pages, the book is an easy read, but the knowledge it provides is invaluable."

—**Gabriel Ciordas,** CEO/founder, Flipsnack

"Creating an online course is like building a bicycle shed; you might think it's easy, until you actually try to do it! Then you realize that there's a steep learning curve, and a serious risk that your first go at it will produce something that just doesn't live up to your high standards. Thankfully, there's an alternative: read *Course Design Formula* by Rebecca Frost Cuevas, do exactly what it teaches, and then celebrate when you find yourself with an online course that is clear, effective, and done a lot sooner than you thought it would be!"

—**Danny Iny,** CEO/founder, Mirasee

"In my many years designing online courses, I have never encountered anything as intuitive and easy to follow as the Course Design Formula. This will become my go-to formula to design courses from now on."

—**Mauricio Cadavid, Ed.D.**, senior instructional designer for California State University, San Bernardino

"The online course community needs this! It's engaging, thought-provoking, and compels you to keep reading. If you're like me, there are spots where you'll even laugh out loud. I just may to send it to a few 'gurus' from whom I've purchased ineffective courses in the past. I've experienced the magic of creating my own course using Rebecca Cuevas' formula and I can confidently say her stuff works.

—**Cheri Merz**, CEO/founder, Metaprosperity LLC

"If you are looking for an outstanding textbook for a class that teaches how to design and deliver online learning, this book is for you and your students. It presents a learning design process that is informed by a deep understanding of the research, presented in a clear and logical way. It can serve as a springboard to help readers understand highly practical and relevant research findings about learning, media, and process. From there, readers can easily launch either into a deeper investigation of salient lines of research or move right into the production of online learning resources—from individual learning objects to full-length courses."

—**Brian Newberry, Ph.D.**, instructional designer, Jackson College

"In the information age, creating cognitively and socially engaging educational content continues to become increasingly important. Rebecca Frost Cuevas synthesizes principles of learning theory, instructional technology, visual design, and usability to create a clear approach to developing your online course. Each of these topics are addressed in other publications, but I have not seen them integrated into an action plan for online teaching and learning as effectively as Ms. Cuevas has done in this book. Her formula is brilliant. This is a must-read for anyone who wishes to teach online."

—**Suzanne Ama, M.S.,** Education, professor of digital media arts

"I could not put the book down. It's an easy read and shows how much knowledge Rebecca has about the subject. In my experience, if someone can make a subject simple and fun, it is because they have a mastery over it. I highly recommended this book! It's an absolute delight and a must-read for online course creators."

—**Neerja Ahuja,** principal consultant and director, Ayurveda Awareness Centre (Perth, Australia)

"Rebecca provides a wealth of knowledge on instructional design. This is a fabulous read for anyone interested in teaching anything. I can't wait to put it into practice."

—**Alison Cameron,** economic development professional, City of Santa Cruz

"This is the book I wish I'd had when I was one of the campus instructional design mentors in Tennessee. This is the book I would have gifted to my entire team when I was the instructional design manager at a tech company, leading a team of twenty designers, most of whom were "accidental" instructional designers with subject expertise but no course development experience. This is a book that can be used in the corporate space, higher education, or by individuals who desire to share their own expertise online for fun or for profit. Each chapter has clearly defined objectives, real-life examples that readers can relate to, and most importantly, a wealth of resources to help the new or seasoned designer assess, design, and review their course idea and learning outcomes. This is by far, one of the best books I have read on course development in years."

—**Mary Nunaley, Ms.ED.**, ATD Master Instructional Designer™, founder of the Lavender Dragon Team, LLC

COURSE DESIGN FORMULA®

....

HOW TO TEACH ANYTHING TO ANYONE ONLINE

REBECCA FROST CUEVAS

Art credits appear on page 419.

Learn and Get Smarter, Inc.
P.O. Box 5238
Riverside, CA. 92517
www.learnandgetsmarter.com
info@learnandgetsmarter.com

Course Design Formula® is a trademark of Learn and Get Smarter, Inc.

Cover design by Gus Yoo
Editing and production by Stephanie Gunning
Book Layout © Book Design Templates
Author photo by Virginia Shaffer Fesunoff, @DarkRmPro

Special discounts are available on quantity purchases by corporations, associations, and others. For details, contact the publisher.

Library of Congress Control Number 2019910513

ISBN 978-1-7327823-1-0 (paperback)
ISBN 978-1-7327823-2-7 (kindle ebook)

Course Design Formula/Rebecca Frost Cuevas —1st ed.

CONTENTS

For my online students—and yours

INTRODUCTION

This is a book about how to create online courses that really teach, at a deep level. It's about how to create courses that people will finish, get results from, and talk about to their friends. It's about how to create courses that make a profound difference in people's lives.

This book will give you the background knowledge necessary to understand why it's important to use an instructional design process to build your course and teach you a step-by-step course design process that will make your courses truly stand out from the crowd.[1] You can begin using this process immediately. On my website, you also can find a set of free materials to help you get started (see "Next Steps").

I've distilled a lifetime of professional training, experience, and research into creating products and services to help you shape your expertise into courses that achieve the goals you have for them. If you read this book, take my signature course, and use my workbooks, you will have the knowledge, skills, and tools to effectively outline any course, on any topic, *in an hour.*

I know this assertion may sound too good to be true. It may sound like pie in the sky. I wouldn't believe it either if I hadn't created the Course Design Formula® myself and tested it with over one hundred experts like you, creating courses on all kinds of topics. Plain and simple, it works!

This book will help you understand what the Course Design Formula® is and why it works. (*Spoiler alert:* It works because it's based on research into how people best learn the exact type of material your course teaches.)

An online course can help you make money because it is infinitely scalable. We all want and need to make money, but our focus at the moment is not on how to make money with online courses. *This book is about how to make a difference with online courses.* The difference you will make lies in setting up your courses to promote powerful learning.

The Course Design Formula® you'll learn to implement in this book will help you design excellent courses to teach anything to anyone in a way that is fun, easy, effective, and fast. The formula cuts through the stress, confusion, and overwhelm many experts face as they try to figure out how to structure their course material.

The quality of an online course depends on its ability to deliver the transformation it promises. And that, in turn, depends on its ability to deliver learning. We'll talk in depth in this book about what real learning involves, how to make it happen, and how specifically to make it happen in your online course. By the end, you'll have the ability to quickly and easily create high-quality learning products that will appeal to your target audience.

I know how hard it is to create an online course— how much work, blood, sweat, and tears go into creating one. I know how deeply you care about helping people learn. My passion is to help you understand the principles of online course design that will lead to the outcomes you desire for your students and yourself: happy students who love what they are getting out of your course, can't wait for your next one, gladly provide you with recurring income, and act as evangelists promoting your courses to everyone they know.

This scenario is win/win/win: Your students will get the learning and transformation they signed up for. You will get professional recognition, financial rewards, and deep fulfillment. And you know who will get the third win? The internet, and society as we know it: because we all will truly be helping each other learn and get smarter and helping make the world a better place.

Now that we're clear on what we're trying to do and why it's important to do it, how do we get there? We get there through understanding the underlying principles of how people learn, and how to design courses that use those principles to help people learn.

There's an infinite number of courses you could teach, each addressing different subject matter for different learners with different goals. Once you grasp the underlying principles of what makes for a great online learning experience, you will be able to teach any course your background and training qualify you for, online. You'll be able to deliver powerful online learning with confidence and skill.

It's not enough for you to know the subject matter. You also have to know how to teach it effectively in the online learning space. In this book I am going to show you how to help your target audience learn the subject matter easily, permanently, and well.

And another thing . . . about that money I mentioned earlier? It's not only important for you to earn the money you deserve from teaching your courses, it's also important for you to save money you don't need to spend to get your courses set up. Once you understand the principles of how people learn, you won't need expensive materials or complex tools to make your courses stand out.

The end product of an online course is not fancy multimedia artifacts. The end product of an online course is learning.

Great learning happens because of great learning design. You don't need fancy tools to design great learning. You just need to understand what makes learning great. Once you know that, you can build amazing courses using simple tools.

In fact, simple tools often can be the best ones, because fancy bells and whistles sometimes get in the way of learning.[2] The focus should not be on the tools you use or the interface your course is nestled in. Neither of those things is what makes your course beautiful. What makes your course beautiful is the learning your students get from it—the knowledge, transformation, and skills.

And that's what I am going to teach you how to produce—not just for one course, one time, but for any course about any subject delivered anywhere and anytime.

What to Expect from This Book

This book distills my forty years of instructional design and teaching experience into a plan of action for creating your stellar online course. You'll get the benefit of what I've learned from earning two master's degrees in education and from creating public education programs that reached over 150,000 learners and won national awards. I've spent the past twelve years researching how to take great offline learning strategies and make them work well in the online space. I've created a research-based system, the Course Design Formula®, that cuts through the chaos and overwhelm to help you design any course fast and well.

Together, we will explore what works to help people learn. We will look at what I've discovered about what does not work, so you can save time, effort, and money as you create your own courses. We will:

- Look at how people learn.
- Clarify what outstanding teachers do to ensure their course participants learn.
- Explore how you can do what outstanding teachers do, in the online teaching space.

- Create a practical plan of action that you can use to design an unlimited number of online courses.

Who Is This Book For?

This book is for those whose passion is to serve others by creating quality online learning experiences. It's for those who believe they will fulfill their life purpose by providing the highest and best learning experiences for their target audiences. It's for experts and entrepreneurs who are dedicated to helping their customers, clients, and course participants learn and grow.

Is this book for you? Here's how you can tell. When you think of your pain point—the thing that causes you stress and makes you lose sleep at night—is it this?

I can't figure out how to provide the highest and best quality online learning experience for my course participants. I want to share my knowledge, wisdom, and insight in ways that transform people's lives. I have a passion to reach people as an online educator and need help doing it. —You, if this book is for you

If those, or similar, ideas resonate with you, then you have come to the right place.

How You May Be Feeling Right Now

If you're like a lot of the experts I work with, you may be feeling frustrated, stuck, and overwhelmed by your course creation project. You have so much expertise to share, and it's important to present it in a way that honors your professionalism and authority in your field. You care deeply about this material; it's your life's work. Many of my students and clients are cutting-edge thought leaders in their fields, which means that the ideas and systems they want to teach are not yet familiar to the general public. It can feel completely overwhelming trying to shape your expertise into an online course that does justice to the dynamism and complexity of the content you want to share. Many experts and entrepreneurs spend years mulling their material over in their minds. They want to create an online course, but the project feels so amorphous and overwhelming that it never gets off the ground.

Now imagine that there was a simple, step-by-step process that could take away all your stress and overwhelm. Instead of going around and around in your own mind, trying to figure out the best way to present your material in an online course, you could have a high-quality learning product designed, built, and ready to go in less time than you ever thought possible. When I work with my private coaching clients, I take them from the state of mind I just described to a complete course outline so quickly that they're amazed. Not only that—they end up loving the resulting course design.

So, if you've been dreading going through your existing content and media to try to shape it into an online course, lay your dread aside. Take a deep breath. Imagine there's a treasure chest sitting just to the right of your workspace. Visualize yourself putting all your existing content into this treasure chest for the time being. Your content will be there ready for you to layer into your course once you have your course structure in place (which won't take long). But you can't actually design an effective online course structure by starting from your existing content. This is especially true if you've been teaching this material in an offline context.

What I learned, the hard way, is that you can't just take an effective offline course, digitize it, and end up with an effective online course. Instead, you need to start by designing a new course structure that works specifically for online learning. And that requires you to (temporarily) let go of what you know works offline.

In this book, I will teach you to apply a research-based design process to the goal of creating an elegant and effective online course structure that you are going to love. (I promise!)

Who I Am and Why I Wrote This Book

I have always been a teacher. After my first day of kindergarten, I lined up all my stuffed animals and taught them everything I'd learned in school that day, and I've been teaching, in some form, ever since.

I earned a bachelor's degree in English from Harvard, and two master's degrees in education. My first master's, from Wheelock College Graduate School, is in curriculum design and development. My second, from California State University, San Bernardino, is in instructional technology.

For over forty years, I've taught people of different ages ranging from toddlers to senior citizens. I've taught English and foreign languages. I've taught advanced meditation techniques. I've taught values and ethics. I've taught about water and wastewater and electricity and resource conservation.

For fifteen years I designed and developed education programs for public agencies in Southern California. The education programs I created reached thousands of students in twelve school districts and won national awards. But more important to me than either numbers or awards were the letters I received from the teachers and students who participated in those education programs. Over a fifteen-year period, I received physical letters from the many thousands of students whose teachers had encouraged them to write to me after my school visits. In these letters, students shared the impact that my programs had on them, the insights they had gained from the learning activities I provided, and how those insights made them feel. They shared what they had learned and why it mattered to them. And that is what mattered to me.

In 2007, I decided to take my existing in-person education programs and put them online. I thought the transition would be smooth. The in-person education programs were effective and well-received. I had delivered them in hundreds of classrooms to rave reviews. Everything had been thoroughly tested. School administrators, teachers, and students praised them. I really thought it would be easy to put them online.

I was wrong.

When I set out to actually do that, I discovered that it was not easy at all. Sure, it was easy to create a digital version of a face-to-face teaching experience. But it was not easy to replicate the level of engagement and interaction I already knew how to achieve in person.

What I discovered the hard way is that you can't just turn an existing face-to-face lesson into a series of digital files, put those files online, and create a great learning experience. This is true for people who are already highly trained and experienced teachers. For someone who has never taught in the real world (and so needs to first learn how to teach at all and *then* learn how to teach online)—it's even harder.

The good news is that the methods I am going to share with you in this book will help you create an effective online course that promotes deep learning from the beginning, whether you are already an experienced teacher in offline settings or just starting out.

In my second master's project, I spent seven years grappling with the question of how to design effective and engaging online instruction. I tried things that seemed intuitive to me as an experienced educator and found they did not work the same way online. I ran into many roadblocks and obstacles while trying to do what I already knew how to do in the physical classroom space. I worked hard at figuring this out, so you won't have to!

Finally, I discovered a method that works to quickly design effective, engaging instruction in the online space. I developed that method into the Course Design Formula® that I'm about to share with you in this book.

Why This Book Is Needed Now

I am on a mission to transform the way people teach and learn online. My vision is to light up the planet, one mind at a time. My strategy is to help you become an inspired online educator by creating "light-bulb moments" for your course participants.

The Democratization of Online Course Creation

It used to be that courses and training materials could only be created by specialized agencies (textbook publishers, school districts, and organizations with large marketing and training budgets). But that is no longer the case. While individual teachers and parents have always created learning materials for their own students and children to use, now, for the first time, individuals can independently create and publish courses that have the potential to reach a worldwide audience.

What's happening today is that the internet and online platforms for blogging and course creation have made it possible for anyone and everyone to create an online course. This is an exciting trend! I am all for it.

But while it's exciting that now everyone has the opportunity to create online courses and share what they know, it's also problematic. Teaching is an art, a science, and a skill. It takes time and training (and some might argue, a degree of inborn talent) to be a great teacher. Nowadays we have a medium (the internet) that allows everyone to teach online. But if that teaching is not informed by the art, science, skill, and talent required to teach well, how much of our desired messages are getting through?

Here is a shocking statistic. While many people sign up for online courses, such as massive open online courses (MOOCs) from renowned institutions, fully 90 percent don't finish them. And some don't even start.[3] Even skilled, professional course creators in the online space, with huge budgets, face challenges in making sure their students actually complete the courses in which they've enrolled—both for free and also when they've paid good money for them. It seems that when it comes to online learning, a lot of people are buying the pretty package, but not all of them are opening the box, and even fewer are consuming all the contents.

And there's an even more challenging problem, which is the one I want to address in this book specifically. What if you are already a skilled teacher, trainer, or presenter in classroom settings and now you want to start teaching online? Or, what if you have never taught before, and now you are faced with the challenge of learning how to teach while learning how to teach online?

In the first case, you know what good teaching looks like. You know that amazing feeling when your student or class or an entire auditorium filled with lecture attendees suddenly gets it. You know the joy of seeing a metaphorical light bulb turn on above your students' heads. Now you want to create that same "aha" experience and that same level of learning for your students, online. But you don't (yet) know how to create those light-bulb moments in the online space.

In the second case, you need to learn how to reach people so you can begin to create light-bulb moments—from scratch. And then you need to learn how to create light-bulb moments online. (The good news is that this book will teach you how to do both at once!)

The principles you'll learn in this book will save you the frustration that I went through of trying to do things that work in a physical classroom but don't work online.

This book will give you a series of shortcuts to quickly get to what does work to create learning and engagement online.

The Course Design Formula® will help you create a high-quality online course that delivers powerful learning fast. Instead of spending months or even years thinking about your course—the whole while with nothing to show for it—you will have an actual course that you can use to establish your authority, share your expertise, and make the difference you are here to make in the world. Your course is the vehicle through which you will transform other's lives, and the Course Design Formula® gives you the insights and resources you need to become the transformative global teacher you have it in you to be.

The Changing Economy

Two trends have been going on at the same time in our society. The traditional job market has become much less secure than it used to be, with companies closing, people getting laid off, benefits and pensions being cut, and jobs becoming harder to find and land. Skilled professionals in their twenties, thirties, and forties with college degrees can take more than a year to find jobs in their own fields—if they ever do find one.

And for older workers, the situation is far worse. Workplaces are replacing full-time benefited positions with part-time positions, adjunct positions, and contract positions that offer no security or job benefits. Work in the real world has become harder to find, harder to keep, and less financially rewarding—with fewer salaried positions and people working longer hours for less pay.

At the same time, the internet beckons with the prospect of earning money—lots of money—for relatively little work. The promise of earning lots of money for little work is an illusion, promoted to get you to buy into whatever is being sold. Lots of money for little work is no truer in the online marketplace than anywhere else . . . at least, not in the *ethical* online marketplace. But the promise still attracts many people, especially when the real-world market offers such a harsh alternative.

Those who enthusiastically choose to be entrepreneurs are excited because the internet gives them a powerful mechanism to make contact with their prospective clients and customers, delivering products and services and communicating even from distant locations.

So, what has grown up is a cottage industry in online course creation. The idea of being able to work from home, spend more time with your family, avoid the hassle and expense of long commutes, and make money twenty-four hours a day, seven days a week, on your own terms is certainly appealing. And seriously, what is wrong with that idea? Nothing! It's a great idea, as long as it actually works out.

For many people, it *does* work out.

I hope that you will be one of them.

The purpose of this book is to give you the tools you need to become one of those successful online course creators—not just for one specific course, but for any course you might ever want to create.

Advances in Technology

Advances in technology have made it possible for anyone with access to the internet to share their message with anyone anywhere in the world via multiple platforms. These platforms keep getting better, more connected, easier to use, and more social every day.

Those are exciting trends. The internet is like a giant global web of neurons connecting mind to mind. As a result, the brain of humanity as a whole is getting more connected and smarter. Each of us is a synapse in that giant global brain, and now we have the means to find our counterparts, connect with others, access research, and home in on topics of interest in ways that would have been unthinkable merely a few years ago.

Not only can we learn from those who have knowledge and wisdom to share with us, but we can reach out to those who are ready and willing to learn from us—people eager to benefit from the wisdom, training, and experience that we ourselves have to share.

Advancing technology also has a downside that you must be aware of as an online course creator. If your course design is so dependent on the technological platform you use that it can't survive outside that platform, your course will become obsolete very quickly as the technology changes, which is happening at lightning speed. To some degree, this cannot be avoided. Technology is going to change. But if your course is built on a solid blueprint of instructional design, you will be able to keep reinventing it to adapt to technological changes.

In other words, *don't mistake the form or format of your course for its substance.*

The substance of your course is not the specific multimedia artifacts you have created. The substance of your course is not videos, audios, PDFs, or worksheets. And the substance of your course is also not the platform the course is embedded in, whether that is your own website or a course platform, such as Thinkific, Teachable, Canvas, Kajabi, Moodle, or any other. All of those are helpful containers that can hold the substance of your course. But the substance of your course itself is the knowledge you impart through it.

The real container for that knowledge needs to be the steps of the instructional design you've created to hold the course together. That container (your instructional design blueprint) is not going to change.

Technology can and certainly will change. But if your instructional design is solid, it will be easy for you to transfer the substance of your course into newer technology containers, as needed in the future, without disrupting the course as a whole.

Baby Boomers

The huge population of Baby Boomers (those who were born between approximately 1946 and 1964, according to the U.S. Census Bureau) are moving into their retirement years.[4] More and more people are looking to turn their professional knowledge and life experience into a resource that will continue earning income during retirement.

Many members of this large cohort have had high-powered careers and want to share their knowledge and wisdom with the world. But they may not have had the time, training, or focus required to transfer that knowledge to the online teaching space.

In his famous article "Digital Natives, Digital Immigrants," Mark Prensky makes a critically important point: Many of those designing instruction today have been shaped by a world completely different from the one their students live in.[5] This makes it hard for educators to design instruction that speaks to learners in their own language.

Prensky's article was written in 2001. But his point about the technology gap between teachers and students is even more compelling today than it was then.[6]

Adding to the dichotomy between digital immigrants (Baby Boomers) and digital natives (Generation X and Millennials), the post-Millennial generation born around the turn of the millennium, Generation Z, has been described as taking this paradigm a step further by being "social natives."[7]

As educators, we need to design and deliver instruction that captures and holds student interest. Prensky is an expert in the area of game design, and his suggestion for meeting learners where they live by designing engaging video games, certainly holds merit. However, that is not an option that is open to most small, independent, online course designers today.

Complicated high-tech multimedia tools are not a requirement for making online teaching engaging. Certainly, if you have the skills, background, tools, resources, and ability to create such games, by all means go for it. However, even the most exciting video game will not deliver true learning unless it is specifically designed to do so. Unless instructional design principles based on how people learn and how the brain works to process new information are built into its design, even the most fun and engaging video game will not deliver true learning.

One of the challenges of delivering learning in the tech space has been the astronomical cost of creating engaging games and simulations. Such projects require complex high-level creative teams. Additionally, it can take so long to develop these games that the technology they were originally designed for becomes obsolete by the time the projects are done.

I once worked with a team that had created a paper-based correspondence course. We wanted to put the course online. A proposal was made to do that for us, using an attractive high-tech design concept that would have cost $100,000 to complete. We did not have that kind of money in our budget, nor was it worth it to us to devote those resources to that project, had we had them. I ended up designing the project myself using Moodle, a free open-source learning management system. These days, the technology that was offered to us at that time for a steep price has become available to anyone for a few dollars a month via various online platforms.

It's exciting to see the developments in video games and virtual-reality simulations that are being developed by large companies with big, multispecialty teams. But as one-person online course designers, that is not you or me. We need to design excellent online instruction using skills and tools we already have, can easily learn to use, and can afford. Not only that, but the more complex technological bells and whistles a site contains, the more places there are for things to go wrong. Improperly designed multimedia tools can even add unnecessary complexity and distraction to an online course.

It's the instructional design that has to be top of the line, not the tech tools.

Our tech tools just have to be good enough to get the job done.

This book will help experts, including those who are "digital immigrants," design effective online instruction for "digital natives," even without fancy and expensive high-tech tools.

To Keep the Internet Fabulous

Do you remember when it was exciting to go to your mailbox or email inbox? Back in the day when "snail mail," and later email, were new, you could count on receiving personal messages that had real value, from people and organizations you cared about.

Nowadays, though, many people dread going to the mailbox, because it's filled with paper junk mail that has to be tossed out—or even shredded (at added expense and inconvenience to you, to protect your privacy). It's a waste of paper, we're cutting down the forests, we're filling the landfills . . . and all for the purpose of allowing strangers to entice us to buy things we don't want or need.

And email is no better. The relentless march of autoresponders addressing us by name can make us feel pulled in too many directions, bombarded by offers and requests and demands. At a certain point, something that was once special and exciting started to feel like a burden, a chore, an imposition, something we want to avoid.

One reason online courses have become a "thing," is that people love the promise of learning something new, especially in a subject that has meaning and value for them. We all want access to products and services that help us achieve our goals. We love shiny packages that promise to deliver transformations that will make our lives better: whether by teaching us how to get fit and find a mate, or by teaching us how to do our jobs better, make more money, or do something we enjoy that makes us feel happy and fulfilled.

But what happens if we sign up (and pay) for online course package after package, only to find that when we open the package, it doesn't contain what we were hoping to get out of it? That's one problem that could happen, but I don't think it's the main one. I think that most online course creators are hardworking and sincere, and truly do their best to deliver on the promises they make. And I think that most online students recognize and appreciate that. But I think there is a dirty little (or big) not-so secret in the online course market right now, one that many buyers of online courses may not be mentioning or complaining about because they think the problem is their own. (It's not.)

Far too many consumers of online courses are having the experience of buying a course, and then either not completing the lessons or completing them but not getting the transformation they had hoped for out of the course. Both of those problems can be solved through the application of better instructional design.

The Human Cost of Poor Instructional Design

In his wonderful book *The Design of Everyday Things*, Donald Norman points out that when something doesn't work right, we as users of that object or device tend to blame ourselves.[8] We assume the item is fine and there's something wrong with us for not being able to figure out how to make it work. But that is often not the case. Often the item really is poorly designed.

Poorly designed objects and tools are not just dangerous, they make us feel bad about ourselves. They make us feel incompetent and unintelligent and inept. And that's what a poorly designed door handle can do. Now think about a poorly designed course that someone purchased to promote their survival or wellbeing, or to achieve an important goal in their life.

If the course does not "work" due to improper learning design, the student is going to feel foolish, incompetent, and inept in multiple ways. They might feel foolish for having invested in something that didn't work. Now they still haven't achieved the transformation they were looking for, and they are out a sum of money. But more than that, they may feel that they are incapable of learning or that the goal they were so eager to achieve is beyond their reach.

And worst of all, they may conclude that online learning simply doesn't work.

If enough people have that type of experience enough times, the market for online courses will end up like snail mail and email: oversaturated with junk that no one wants. Instead of being excited about the possibility of achieving their goals and making their lives better through online courses, people will simply groan when they see another online course advertised in their email inboxes, heading their way like a giant piece of junk mail, promising a transformation they no longer believe is achievable.

If we promise to deliver a transformation to our learners, we have an ethical obligation to deliver on that promise. Good instructional design is what makes the learning that creates the promised transformation, possible.

As I see it, we are standing at a critical time in the market for online courses. We can either design our courses well (so that they deliver on the promises they make) or see the market for online courses dry up because people don't get the value out of those courses, that they want.

To Make Education Great Again

Why does education need to be made great again? Is education not great now? And was education, in fact, ever great in the past?

It's hard to make pronouncements about the state of education as a whole, because education has so many moving parts. There are independent adult learners. There are business trainees. There are families, and teachers, schools and school districts, and communities, and local and state governments, and national education policy. There are scientific research studies and government policy and funding decisions, which sometimes make the educational experiences of learners better and sometimes make them worse.

Education could be great in one community that has ample resources, concerned parents, and enlightened educational leadership, and terrible in another community, right next door, that has none of these. So, while many factors go into making education either great or not so great, one thing stands out: the teacher.

If you think back on your own educational experiences, you are likely to recall some that truly were great and others that were not—even in the same school. What made the difference? Your teacher. The key factor in making an educational experience great for your online course participants is also you, the teacher.

With online learning, you have the opportunity to reach your learners directly, one on one. While schools and school districts do use online learning, this book was written for the teacher, directly. It is for the person who is actually designing the online course, and with online education you can design a course within the larger structure of an educational organization, or all on your own. Either way, the thing that is going to make education great for your learners, is their direct experience of how you teach your course.

No matter what is going on all around us in terms of the education milieu, policy, and so on, the one thing that matters most is how you design the learning experience to promote the transformation you are promising your student.

People come to school, whether online or offline, to make their lives better. The students who are facing the most challenging circumstances are the ones who most need what you have to offer. As an educator, you are a point of light, drawing your students towards a greater light. The soundness of your instructional design is what determines whether your students will or won't be able to reach that greater light of new skills, new opportunities, and new understanding.

To Preserve and Pass on Knowledge

How do we make education great? We design instruction the right way, so students actually learn. We make education great one course, one teacher, and one student at a time.

As more and more teaching moves online (a development that I personally think is wonderful), the quality of instruction in the online space becomes more critical.

Here's where you come in. The huge scale and scope of this problem is clear, but how does it relate to your specific course? You are creating your course in a digital format. That is the form of your course, its outer appearance. *But it is not the substance of your course, its inner truth.*

The inner truth of your course is its instructional design. Instructional design provides the skeleton, the structure that enables your course to stand up on its own.

The outer form of your course may change. Maybe it started as a face-to-face classroom course, presentation, or training . . . and now you want to put it online. Or maybe you put it online on one platform and now you want to move it to a different one. Either way, if you are too attached to the outer form of your course, you won't be able to see through to its bare-bones structure, which is the essential core of your course. If you get too attached to the outer form of your course—the form it appears in at any one time—you won't be able to recreate it easily in another format or another medium should the need arise.

You've worked hard for the knowledge you are sharing in your course. You have something special to offer that other people want and need. The goal of this book is to help you get so strong, solid, and clear on exactly what you are teaching and exactly how people can most easily learn it, that you won't be dependent on any specific platform or medium to get your message across. If it's well-designed, you could teach your course on multiple platforms or move it from one to another with ease. You can change the media to adapt to different learning situations or different learner needs. Understanding the bare bones structure of your course from an instructional design point of view will enable you to recreate your course with relative ease.

The principles this book teaches will give you the equivalent of x-ray glasses to look inside any course, understand how it's put together, and see where you need to make modifications and changes so the course will stand up better. Once you can do that, your ability to pass on knowledge to others won't depend on any specific medium, context, or platform. You will be platform-independent, able to make the necessary modifications to teach what you know with confidence to any audience, in any medium, anywhere. That's a promise.

To Save Civilization from the Darkness That Is Closing in All Around Us

Why am I being so melodramatic? Because these are the actual stakes. The dark ages didn't happen due to a lack of knowledge about science and philosophy. They happened because that knowledge stopped being passed on. The purpose of education is to pass on knowledge so that people can learn new skills, make their lives better, and keep moving forward.

Ineffective teaching, whether in classrooms or online, puts our society at risk.

- If no one learns how to set up electrical wiring or maintain a power plant, the lights go out.
- If no one learns medicine, people get sick and die.
- If no one learns psychology, we stop understanding ourselves and each other.
- If no one learns conflict resolution, small battles turn into big ones . . . or even into wars.
- If no one learns science, we lose hundreds of years of progress that have improved the quality of life for people all over the world.
- And if no one learns history, then as the saying goes, we are doomed to repeat it.

Now, your online course might not be life-altering on a grand scale. Maybe you just want to teach someone how to improve their tennis serve. The future of civilization as we know it does not depend on whether or not they learn that from you.

True.

But your future may depend on it, and so may that of your course participants.

If the topic of your course is important enough for you to devote long hours to creating it, and for your students to devote long hours to learning from it, then it is important enough to do it right.

It's the principles and practices of proper instructional design that make it possible to pass on knowledge—any kind of knowledge—to new learners.

How do we fight the darkness that is closing in all around us? The difference between light and darkness is a properly designed electrical circuit. When you design instruction, you are in fact building a circuit through which information can flow from your mind to your student's mind. If the circuit is built right, the information will flow, and the light will go on.

If the circuit is built poorly, nothing will happen (or worse yet, you will create a short circuit through information overload). Your student will burn out from trying to make the light switch (your course) produce understanding that is simply not happening. Eventually your student will give up and walk away. And if enough students do that, people all over the world will say, "Online education doesn't work. I tried it but I didn't learn anything. It's a waste of money and time."

If people give up on education, the lights will go out all over the world. It's happened before. It's up to us not to let it happen again. So yes, I am being melodramatic—because the stakes really are that high.

The future of civilization depends on the transmission of knowledge. The transmission of knowledge is happening, to a greater and greater extent, online. You, as an online course designer, are one of the ones making this transmission happen. Therefore, you need to design your circuits properly so the lights can go on in your students' minds.

This book will teach you how to design those circuits properly.

And that is why you need this book.

What This Book Will Do for You

This book will save you time, money, and energy and spare you from frustration as you set up your online course. It will teach you research-based principles of how people learn, and what effective teaching does to ensure that people learn. It also will help you understand how effective teaching in the online space differs from effective teaching conducted face to face. This will be especially helpful to you if you are an experienced face-to-face teacher or presenter and now you want to teach online with the same level of elegance, effectiveness, and grace.

If you've never taught at all in any context, this book will help you start out on the right footing by designing your online course for the way people learn best.

So, let's begin!

PART ONE

BIG IDEAS ABOUT LEARNING
AND TEACHING ONLINE

ONE

....

WHAT IS LEARNING?

At a biological level, learning is the process of adapting to our environment in ways that promote survival, which means that learning is the most important activity that any living thing can do. Because learning is critical to our survival, the brain imposes strict requirements on how we learn. The brain only wants to let new material into its long-term storage area (where the items we have learned stay) if that new information promotes our well-being and survival.

If the brain can't tell if new information is good to let into its long-term storage area or not, it's safer to leave it out. Which brings us to the central questions this book is designed to answer.

- What is learning, and how can we tell if it's happening?
- Are people actually learning what they're trying to learn?
- Are we helping people learn effectively, online?

Let's visit the vast warehouse where the brain processes and stores information. Follow me on an imaginary journey inside the brain!

What It Actually Takes to Learn Something

Welcome to the inside of the brain! Here we are, literally at the nerve center of human learning.

The brain has *one* job, and it's a doozy: to keep us alive. Talk about responsibility.

Keeping in mind that this visit is a metaphor, what are we looking at here? We're visiting the part of the brain that processes new information and organizes it for future use, and we're looking at the place where new information gets processed and labeled for storage in the brain's long-term "storage vaults."

In this area we see shelves holding containers of various shapes and sizes. As new information comes into the brain, it is processed, labeled, and stored in these mental containers, which are called *schemas*.[1]

Before we take a tour of the brain's schema-storage process, let's see how information gets into this area of the brain to begin with.

The Brain's Narrow Doorway

Let's say that this brain we're visiting belongs to someone who is taking an online course, and they're watching a video that is part of that course, right now. The video is presenting all sorts of new information, because the instructor is a world-class expert in her field. She has a huge amount of valuable information stored in her own brain, and the purpose of the course is to transfer that information to the learner's brain— the very brain we are standing inside of as we take this virtual tour.

As we watch information from the course come hurtling toward us, we notice that there's a lot of information trying to get to us, but it has to come through a very narrow doorway.

Stepping out of our metaphor for a minute, I'll mention that this so-called narrow doorway is *working memory*, the brain's ability to process new information.[2]

The doorway that leads into the brain's long-term information storage area is so narrow that only five to seven pieces of information can fit through it at any one time.[3] But the instructor, a talking head on a video, is talking a mile a minute!

This has been going on for the past half hour, because the student is watching a long talking-head video. Is any of the information from that video actually making it through this narrow doorway into the storage area of the student's brain?

Yes, the first five to seven pieces of information from the instructor's video got through the narrow doorway and were taken to the brain's processing area just inside, to be labeled and stored in those schema containers we were talking about earlier. But while that was happening, more pieces of information kept trying to push in through the doorway, and the brain's processing system couldn't keep up with all of them.

One of the brain's important functions is to keep us alive by tuning out anything that is not essential to our survival. So, when hundreds of pieces of information that are not critical to survival try to flood through its narrow doorway, the brain hits an emergency shut-off valve to tune out the unnecessary stimuli. This is why the student whose brain we're visiting has stopped paying attention to the online course and is currently watching cat videos in another browser window.

What does that mean for you as you create your online course? If you want the information in your course actually to make it into your learners' brains, you need to present the information in small, focused chunks. There's no point presenting more than a few pieces of new information at a time, because only a few pieces of information can pass through a student's narrow brain doorway at a time.

You should also make sure that the information you present in your course is related to something your learners need and care about. People want better health, better relationships, more money, and more time. In order to get your learners' attention and keep them motivated, make it clear how the material you're presenting will improve their lives. For example, right now you are learning how to structure your own online course.

How will this benefit you?

- Getting this right will give you better relationships with your course participants because they'll be grateful to you for helping them really learn.

- Creating an effective course that delivers the transformation it promises will give you more money if more people complete your course, recommend it to people in their social networks, and sign up for your future courses.
- It will increase your productivity by helping you create more and better courses in less time.
- It will improve your health by giving you more time to focus on other things like exercise and sleep.

Do I have your attention now? Is your brain processing this information? I thought so.

In creating an online course, you need to make those types of connections clear for your course participants as well. You need to have their full attention riveted on you before you start to present them with new information. They need to know how your new information will benefit them in ways that promote their survival and well-being.

You need to present them with no more than five to seven pieces of new information at a time, so that the new information can fit through their brain's narrow doorway. And then you need to help them process each piece of new information so it can be stored forever in their long-term memory.

That's a lot of steps for any piece of new information to go through before we can say that it's actually been learned!

Are most online course creators making sure that all those steps take place for the benefit of their students, and in the right order? Not yet—although hopefully after reading this book they will.

The important thing is that you will, because you are learning why it's important to take these steps. And as we continue our journey, I'll show you how to ensure that every piece of information you present in your course gets properly taken in, processed, labeled, and stored in your course participants' brains. In other words, that it gets learned.

Now let's step through the narrow doorway and into the information-processing area of your student's brain to see how a piece of information that makes it through the doorway gets processed, labeled and stored for future retrieval.

Schemas: Mental Containers for Storing Knowledge

Once a new piece of information has passed through the narrow doorway into the brain's storage area, it has to be unpacked, analyzed, sorted, and labeled before it can be stored.[4] That takes a lot of mental work! Schemas help the brain arrange information for easy storage and retrieval by comparing it to other information that is already there. It takes less mental effort to learn something new if we can relate it to something we already know.

That's why metaphors are useful teaching tools. A metaphor makes it easy to relate something new and unknown to something familiar. It gives us a template we can copy as we build a mental storage container to hold new information. I'll be using metaphors throughout this book for this very reason.

It's hard work building a schema from scratch for the first time, but once built, a schema can be used over and over again in different ways. Information can be added to or subtracted from a schema, and schemas can be related to each other in complex ways.

The plural form of *schema* is *schemata*, since this is a Greek word. But I'll use *schemas* as the plural noun in this book because it sounds more natural in English.

As an expert in your subject, you've spent a long time creating many interrelated schemas in your area of expertise. If you now try to transfer everything you've learned directly from your brain into your course participants' brains—without first helping them take in, sort, and process the information step by step so they can build their own schemas to store that information—it's not going to work.

You have to help your course participants unpack, analyze, sort, and label the new information you're presenting if you want them to be able to *really* absorb it. You do that by helping them either fit the new information into their existing mental frameworks, or by helping them build the new frameworks they need to hold the information.

As you create your online course, it's important to think about the following questions.

- What prior knowledge must your course participants have, in order to be able to take in, process, and store the material you're sharing with them?
- Do they already have the schemas they need, so you are now just going to help them put some additional new information into their existing mental storage bins?
- Or are you going to have to help them build entirely new mental storage bins from scratch (which takes more work on the student's part and more guidance from you)?

If you're feeling a bit overwhelmed right now, don't worry. The Course Design Formula® makes it simple and easy to build all these steps into your course creation process. You'll do it the right way without having to stop and think about it. What I'm doing now is providing you with background information that shows why the steps you'll be following to build your course are needed, and why those steps will make your course easy to create and easy to learn from.

In helping people sort and store the new material you're sharing with them, it's critical to keep their prior knowledge in mind. What do they already know that relates to the new material you're teaching them?

As we get further along on this journey we're taking together, I'll show you how to help your course participants access their relevant prior knowledge at every step of your course. The course design process you'll be learning will make it easy for you to see where you need to help your learners build a proper foundation for what you are about to share with them. That way, everything you teach in your online course will make it all the way into your learner's brains—and stay there. The new information you're presenting will get properly labeled and put in the right mental container (schema) where your learners can access it.

When the information you present in your course is stored in your course participants' long-term memory, they have actually learned it.

Let's visit the brain's huge back storage area to see what it (metaphorically) looks like when someone has in fact actually learned something, which means that the new information is now theirs to keep and use forever.

The Brain's Permanent Storehouse of Knowledge

We've squeezed through the narrow doorway of short-term memory that leads into the back storage area of our online student's brain.

We've passed through the processing area where new information is sorted, labeled, related to what the student already knows, and put into containers (schemas) for long-term storage.

Now we're entering the huge, long-term storage area of the brain, where every schema this person has ever built in her life is stored for future retrieval.

This storage area is gigantic! It is mind-bogglingly vast. There actually doesn't seem to be any limit to it. There is no back wall. The shelves and shelves of neatly labeled boxes containing everything this person has learned in their life, seem to go on forever. We actually don't know if there is a practical limit to the amount of information that can be stored in the human brain, relative to how much a person can realistically learn in a lifetime.[5]

Given how huge this storage area is, it seems surprising that the doorway for getting new information in here is so narrow. Why is that? If you think about the even huger amount of sensory information that is constantly impacting us from all sides as we move through the world, you can see that even a gigantic storage area would quickly get filled with junk if there were no filter on what gets in. And then it would be impossible to find the truly important information in the midst of all that junk. (All you have to do is think about your own cloud-storage folders or email inbox to know what I'm talking about, am I right?)

At the moment, we are in the long-term storage area of your online student's brain. There is a lot of information of all kinds stored here. The information is arranged and sorted in useful ways for easy retrieval, with similar types of information stored near each other on neatly labeled shelves.

Let's look for the information from the online course that this student is taking. There's a shelf labeled with the name of the course, but there's hardly anything on that shelf. That's because the student started taking the course, then tuned out of that long talking-head video because too much information was coming at her and she couldn't process it. So, all we see on the shelf for this online course are the first five or seven things the instructor said.

In most online courses, the first five or seven things usually have to do with the course schedule, where to log in, what you're going to get out of the course, and why you should be excited to be there. Then the instructor gets busy talking. But if that talking is not done in a way that promotes learning, the words turn into a blur. The first two or three things the instructor was discussing in that long video I mentioned are here in a box on the shelf, but that's it.

Now, let's hop out of the long-term storage area of this student's brain for a minute and jump into the instructor's brain instead. We're brain-hopping! *Whee!*

OK, *phew,* we landed. We're in the long-term storage area of the instructor's brain, peeking in on her brain while she's teaching her class. Immediately it's evident that the shelf for the subject matter of the online course in the instructor's brain looks totally different from the shelf for this same course in the student's brain.

For the instructor, there's not just one shelf. There's a huge section of the long-term storage area that contains shelves and shelves all filled with neatly labeled containers relating to the subject matter of the online course. That's because the instructor is an expert on this topic. She has spent years gathering information and creating containers to hold that information in this area of her brain.

Now that the instructor is teaching her online course, she's trying to transfer this huge amount of information to her student's brain. That's why she's describing everything she's learned in a lifetime, in one long talking-head video.

The trouble is, that doesn't work. In order to effectively transfer this information, the instructor needs to send just a few things at a time through the narrow doorway that leads into the information processing area of the student's brain.

Even though the instructor has already processed and labeled the information, the student needs to process and label it again for her own brain's storage area. That's because when we process, label, and store information, we relate it to what we already know and then store it according to how our own mind works.

If you've ever had someone else come into your home and "organize" all your stuff and then leave, you'll understand what I'm talking about. Unless your stuff is organized based on the way you are going to look for it and use it after said "helper" is gone, you'll never find anything in there again, no matter how nice it looks. (Don't ask me how I know this.)

The same is true for learning. We learn best when we are able to process, label, and organize new information using our own mental models and our own mental storage and retrieval system.[6]

We have to build schemas ourselves. Learning is only effective when we build our own mental containers to hold new information, label those mental containers with labels that make sense to us, and then store them in a way that will help us find them again.

So, what's an expert to do to help her students? How can we share our expertise with those who want to learn from us? We can do it by implementing processes and procedures that lead to effective teaching.

TWO

....

WHAT IS TEACHING?

There's a difference between telling someone something and teaching it to them. If that weren't the case, we wouldn't hear so many parents lament: "How many times have I told you . . . ?"

The reason parents have to tell their children the same thing so many times is that the child has not actually learned it. One of the main reasons children don't learn from what parents (repeatedly) tell them is that the children are not motivated to learn it. (We will address how to build motivational factors into your learning materials later on.) Another reason people don't learn is that the message is not delivered in ways that maximize learning. From the learner's perspective, there is a difference between learning something and simply being exposed to information.

If we are exposed to more information than we want or are able to absorb, we simply tune it out.

I want to share an example of this from the time I led a youth group. Every week I sent out a long detailed letter to each parent in our youth group. This letter was generally several paragraphs long. It was brimming with information about the upcoming week's activities: where to go, what to bring, and so on—every detail imaginable. And yet to my great surprise, many people were missing important facts. They would show up on the wrong day, at the wrong time, at the wrong place, with the wrong equipment, or not at all. Clearly, something was not working. I was sending the information out, but it wasn't getting into people's brains. People were being exposed to information, but weren't learning it.

Why not? Because many of the dedicated, caring, busy parents whose children were in my group were not reading the long, detailed letters. Or if they were, they were not retaining the details of what to bring to the next group activity.

What could I do to fix this? I needed to give parents something in writing in advance, because if I just called them the night before it would be too late for them to get ready.

Finally, I hit on a solution that worked.

Early in the week, I sent out a postcard with only the most critical information. I highlighted the most important points in bold colors using colored highlighters. I told the parents to put the postcard on their fridge in a prominent place and forget about it. Then, two days before the planned activity, I called each parent and reminded them to go get the postcard off the fridge. I asked them to read it right then and there. I verbally checked in with them to be sure they had what they needed for the activity and were clear on the meeting place and time. If there were any issues and problems, we took care of it together, right there and then.

This system worked because it was both visual (the written information on the postcard) and auditory (our phone conversation). Although I gave parents a long lead time by sending the postcards early in the week, I did not ask them to focus their attention on it until it was almost time for the activity, when the information was directly relevant to them.

The parents knew where to find the information but did not have to process it until it was needed, at which point it became a priority for them. Putting only the most critical information on the cards worked with, rather than against, the limits of their short-term memory.

You may say this sounds like a lot of extra work for me as a group leader.

It was.

Effective teaching takes work up front, but the rewards are worth it.

Mark Twain (among others) has been credited with saying that he once wrote a long letter because he didn't have time to write a short one.[7] A long letter (or long talking-head video) is a first draft. It's useful for getting thoughts out of our heads and onto the page or screen, where we can see them. It helps us look at the contents of our own mental warehouse, so we can see what we want to share with our learners. It's an important first step, but it's only the first of *many* that have to happen in order to promote learning.

There are other steps we have to follow after that to make the material easy for our learners to take in, process and remember. You'll be learning those steps later in this book.

Designing an effective online course requires more preparation up front than teaching the same subject in a classroom. Because your online course materials have to compensate for the fact that you are not there with your students face to face, online course materials have to stand on their own in a way that doesn't apply in a classroom situation.

Similar to my youth group example, online course materials have to be presented in bite-sized pieces in order to get past the limits of short-term memory.[8] That's why my long, detailed letters were not effective, whereas my short, color-coded postcards were.

The goal of this book is to make sure you are aware of the steps that have to happen to make information learnable.

Now, let's get started focusing on how to ensure learning in your online course.

Teaching Means Arranging a Series of Events That Promote Learning

Many people creating online courses today don't perceive what they are doing as teaching. They don't think of themselves as teachers or of their course participants as learners, possibly because they think teaching occurs exclusively in school settings. They mainly view their courses as digital products they can sell, and their course participants as customers who have engaged in a business transaction with them.

An online course can certainly be a tool for business growth. In fact, it generally should be. But once the sale of your product has occurred, your product needs to deliver on its promises. The videos and PDFs in an online course don't work by magic just sitting in the cloud. Paying for them doesn't make the desired transformation happen. Customers won't get anything out of an online course unless they actually use it. And using it means consuming the digital information in a way that produces learning.

Teaching involves presenting new material in a way that allows the brain to process it. If your online course is going to deliver the transformation promised in its marketing materials, you are indeed going to be teaching.

The question at the heart of this book is, how can we apply the art of teaching to creating an online course? We may not have time to get an advanced degree in education and spend years getting hands-on practice teaching in classrooms. Or we may have already done just that, and now want to produce the same level of engagement and effectiveness in an online course that we know how to produce during face-to-face teaching. Whether creating our first online course will be our first time teaching at all, or is our first time teaching online, it is how the learner learns that matters. Our online course must be grounded in the requirements of learning.

In *The Essentials of Learning for Instruction,* educational researcher and theorist Robert M. Gagné, Ph.D., defines instruction as the "arrangement of external events to activate and support the internal processes of learning."[9]

What does that imply for your online course? Here are three definitions to remember.

- *Learning* is the process of taking in new information through the brain's narrow doorway and processing it for long-term storage.
- *Teaching* means arranging a series of events in ways that support learning.
- Therefore, teaching means arranging a *series of events* that support the processing and long-term storage of new information.

What does this mean for you as an online course creator?

It means that in order for your course to deliver real transformation, it's not enough for you to simply tell your course participants what you already know. That would not be teaching, but merely exposing people to information.

In order to teach others what you already know, you must take them through a structured series of steps that make it possible for them to know what you know, for themselves.

THREE

....

HOW TO TEACH EFFECTIVELY ONLINE

In exploring how to design online learning experiences that create the best conditions for learning, we need to factor in what makes the online-learning space special and how it differs from the face-to-face learning space.

Know What You Can and Can't Do Well Online

We are all familiar with classroom, workshop, and lecture-based learning environments; as learners, we've been in and out of these types of learning environments our entire lives.

As online course creators, some of us are familiar with teaching face to face, and others may have never done so. But we all carry the tropes of face-to-face learning with us, from our own education and life experience.

The questions we're exploring are:

- How does the online learning space *differ* from the classroom learning space?
- What can we do *better* in the online learning space, than we can in the classroom?
- What can we do *worse,* or *not at all,* in the online learning space, compared to the classroom learning environment?

The things that a design situation allows the designer to do, are called *affordances.*

The things that a design situation prevents the designer from doing, are called *constraints.*

In this chapter, we are going to explore some of the best practices that masterful teachers use in face-to-face learning environments and consider how to implement those best practices in online learning. But before considering the best practices one by one, we need to be clear on the affordances and constraints of online learning.

If you would like to learn more about affordances and constraints as they relate to design in general, I suggest you read *The Design of Everyday Things* by Don Norman (see Bibliography).

Affordances: What You Can Do Well Online

What does the online learning environment allow you to do better, as you design instruction, than the face-to-face learning environment? The online platform allows you to reach more learners than you could possibly address face to face.

What's the biggest audience you could speak to in person? If you were speaking in a football stadium, you could address a few thousand people.

Online you can reach even more. There is truly no limit to the number of students you can reach online.

Not only that, but via online teaching you can reach each of these unlimited number of people directly, as if you were talking to them one to one. You can interact with your learners in a much closer and more personal way online than you could if you were teaching in a football stadium, or even a lecture hall or classroom.

In addition to interacting with you directly, one to one, the online environment allows your students to interact with the subject matter in very direct ways. Through the proper use of multimedia tools, such as instructional video and images, your online-learning space can direct your students' attention anywhere in the world, solar system, or universe, at any level of magnification. Whether you want your students to focus on a subatomic particle or the vastness of outer space, you can take them there in an instant through the use of properly structured multimedia learning materials.

The key term here is *properly structured.*

Whatever you show your students through online media needs to be carefully designed to be part of a learning sequence that helps learners store this new information in their long-term memory. Unless you are helping your learners build new schemas through proper lesson design, you are not actually teaching them anything, you are just exposing them to pretty pictures.

The online-learning environment affords you the ability to show your students anything you want, but it is up to you as the instructor to make good use of this affordance by designing your lesson so it shows your students the right things, in the right way, in the right sequence, and at the right time.

And what about student-to-student interaction? How does the online-learning environment work to support that? We have all, as a global community, been engaged in a massive social experiment as the internet has evolved—an experiment focused on how technology allows people to interact with each other at a distance. As technology has evolved to the point where communication almost as good as that afforded by face-to-face interaction has become possible with anyone, anywhere, we have discovered that there are both good and bad things about this powerful new tool.

On the plus side, we can make friends with people we never would have met otherwise. We can learn about other places, cultures, and points of view. We can keep up with all our friends at once via social media. We can network with colleagues in remote locations. We can create interest groups, support groups, and research collaboratives around specific topics with others who share our passion for knowledge on any imaginable subject. We have many ways to learn and get smarter together, that we never had before.

But there is a dark side to this new social connectedness that the internet and telecommunications media allow. Aspects of our lives that we formerly could have kept separate sometimes collide now in ways that are not always beneficial. Things we say or do can have unintended consequences. The online social environment magnifies and intensifies the opportunities for communication and social interaction, whether in good or bad ways. Things said and done online don't vanish into the ether afterward. They create a permanent record. Our inability to see each other in person online in the same way we do in real life can lead to missed cues, miscommunications, and misunder-standings.

Online social and emotional interaction is at the same time more intense and permanent, yet also more fleeting and tenuous, than face-to-face interaction. It's as if the social and emotional stakes are higher, yet not as solid, real, or tangible as in real-world social interactions.

Perhaps that's because to the extent we can't fully see and experience each other in online interactions, we fill in the blanks with "information" from our own imaginations. It's easier to project our own thoughts, ideas, wishes, and fantasies onto others when we can't fully see them. It's harder to know the reality of each other when we're not fully "there," in the same space, at the same time, in the same social environment.

Sometimes this works out well. Online, people can get to know each other from the inside out, sharing thoughts, ideas, and insights in ways that are hard to do during in-person interactions—especially with relative strangers, as in a classroom setting.

Maintaining a harmonious social environment is an integral part of the teaching function. As human beings, we are social creatures. We don't learn in a vacuum. Our social and emotional natures are an integral part of the whole person sitting in front of the computer screen. As you design your online course, it's important to keep the social aspects of learning, and the affordances and constraints of the online-learning environment, in mind.

A decision you will need to make is: do you want your students to interact with each other in your online course, or only with you? Or do you only want them to interact with the course materials, and not with other people at all?

How will you define, structure, and manage social interaction? What features of online learning can you use to create the kind of social environment within which you want your learners to operate? What potential obstacles and roadblocks to creating an optimal social-learning environment should you be aware of and deal with proactively, in advance?

Constraints: What You Can't Do Well Online

The price online instructors pay for being able to reach an unlimited number of students is not being physically present with those students in space and time. Removing the need to meet in a single space at a single time makes it possible to reach an unlimited number of students via online teaching. But it also means that you as an online teacher can't see your students directly, and they can't see (the real) you.

This limitation can be lessened by holding meetings such as live hangouts and live video sessions. But then you run into other issues that are part of the online teaching situation: time zone differences, schedule conflicts, and scalability issues.

You can address those issues by recording any synchronous sessions you hold, such as live hangouts, and making the recording available to all students at a later time. It's not a perfect solution, but it's the best that can be done given the constraints of the online-teaching situation.

An issue to think about before sharing replays of live group sessions is whether you want to include video of your course participants talking or show just yourself talking as you answer questions.

From a student's perspective, participating in a video conference or watching a recorded one does not have the same immediacy as attending an in-person lecture, workshop, meeting, or class. It can be extremely boring, and not at all useful, to watch or listen to a recording of other people exchanging pleasantries and addressing questions that are not directly relevant to the subject matter—or not of interest to you personally. What works in a live, synchronous session may not work as well once a recording of that session is put online.

The issue of student privacy also must be considered if recordings of class sessions are put online. Sharing the replay of a live class video may work well in the restricted space of a small live private class, but become problematic in a larger evergreen course.

One way to address this concern of who is being shown speaking on replay videos is to create a written agenda for any live calls and share it with the class ahead of time. Offer students the opportunity to submit any questions they want you to address by a specific deadline before the live video call. Then send out an email to all students before the call, letting them know the topics that will be discussed. This allows all students to participate in the call by submitting their questions in advance—and gives you a chance to plan your answers.

This same method also preserves student privacy, because the resulting video will only show you talking, and will keep the source of the questions anonymous.

One thing good teachers tell students is that the only "dumb question" is the one you don't ask. Any individual member of your class may have a question that speaks to issues a lot of the other students have. Just as in a physical classroom, encouraging students to ask questions helps you as the instructor know where any misconceptions about the subject matter may be lurking in your students' minds.

Allowing students to ask questions (that you will answer directly during the live session) keeps students engaged with the subject matter, and keeps you engaged with your learners' concerns.

You can create a printed transcript of the live call later for students to access. As you teach the same class more than once, you will be able to cull a series of frequently asked questions (FAQs) from these transcripts that you can store in a searchable knowledge base for all students to access. An FAQ section or knowledge base keeps you from having to answer the same question over and over again. This is one way to make good use of the affordances of the online learning space, by storing information in an archive that is searchable.

Creating an archive of FAQs for your students' future use is an example of how you can turn a constraint (the lack of direct face-to-face interaction) into something that works better online than off.

This example illustrates an important point: don't fight the constraints or limitations of the online teaching medium. Instead, make them work for you and your students.

An important part of working with the constraints of online learning is simply being aware of them. Here's an important one that's so all-encompassing it can be hard to notice: online learning has no specific physical reality.

Especially with *asynchronous* online learning— meaning, learning that can be done at any time of the student's choosing—there is nowhere the student has to be, and nothing they have to do at any particular time. There is nothing tangible or concrete to anchor your students' participation in your course to their outer life. (I'm talking now about the kinds of courses you are designing as an independent online instructor. Online courses provided by universities as part of a student's graded enrollment do have deadlines—but yours probably doesn't.)

Many online courses try to get around this by using a timed structure: delivering one lesson per day, one unit per week, a timed email series sent by an autoresponder, and so on. There's nothing wrong with doing this, and it may be the best way to structure and deliver your course. But in real life, a problem sets in if and when (usually when) the student gets behind in the timing sequence. If they miss a day because they were too busy, the next day they have to do two days of work in order to catch up.

And since they were already busy, missing two days makes it even harder to stay on track. Before you know it, they've stopped doing the lessons entirely, and because their participation in the course was entirely voluntary, and there is nothing in their outer physical world to remind them to finish what they started, it's easy to lose them into cyberspace.

You can counter this problem by providing students with something concrete and tangible to place in their physical environment that reminds them to stay on track with your course and helps them complete it.

The best time and place to do this is at the very beginning of your course.

You can provide a downloadable PDF of the course schedule, with boxes students can check off as they complete each lesson. This can be printed out and placed on the refrigerator, a mirror, bulletin board, notebook, or somewhere else the student can see it.

You can also provide them with a notebook cover page to slip into the plastic sheet on the front of a binder that you have them set up at the beginning of the course.

Students may drop out of your course's carefully planned time sequence if one of your lessons is too difficult or challenging, leading the student to put it aside for later. If they do that, they may never come back. In a physical classroom you would notice your students sitting at their desks staring into space not doing anything, but you can't see that in an online course.

There are two ways to counter this issue using your course design. First, make sure your students will be able to successfully complete each lesson, as long as they follow through, step by step. You'll get tools to ensure they can, as you continue through this book.

Second, create some kind of feedback mechanism where students have to submit something every day or week or after every lesson. Set things up so that if they don't submit the required item by the deadline, they get an automatically sent email from you asking what's wrong and what help you can provide to help them stay on track.

Learning something new is hard work because it requires that we step outside our comfort zones and actually change our brains. If we haven't stepped outside our comfort zones and changed our brains, we haven't actually learned anything new, we've just been exposed to information.

It's natural for all of us to resist stepping outside our comfort zones and to resist change. Your students want to make the changes your course promises, but it's hard for them to do. If it were not hard, the changes would not be real. And if it were not hard, they would not be paying you to help them do it. Your job as a teacher is to take those hard changes and make them as easy and doable as possible—and then to monitor the extent to which your students are following through on making the changes. You have to know if and when your learners are stuck, so you can help them get unstuck.

The online environment makes it easy for students to sign up for change, but hard for them to follow through, because it's so easy just not to show up and do the work.

So, to summarize:

- **Make the work as easy to do as possible.** You will learn how in Part Two of this book.

- **Create feedback mechanisms** to ensure your students are showing up and doing the work. We'll go into that in Part Two as well.
- **Use physical, tangible reminders** of the commitment learners have made to your course, that you refer to in every lesson. That way, by the end of the course they will have a completed physical notebook of course notes, drawings, completed workbook pages, checked off checklists, or some other tangible (offline) reminder of the progress they have made toward achieving their own goals in your course.

We've touched on some of the things the online learning environment makes it easy or hard for us to do as educators. Now let's look at some of the things that make your course material either easy or hard for your learners to understand.

Making Your Course Easy to Understand: Cognitive Load Theory

Learning anything new, at any age, has a certain amount of difficulty built into it. That's because when we learn something new, we are actually changing our brains.

And the brain, like everything else in the world, resists change.

Things resist change in order to maintain their integrity. If everything was open to changing all the time, the world would be a shapeless mass of gelatinous goo in which nothing would hold its shape or maintain its structural integrity. If you want to change your brain, you have to overcome its built in resistance to change.

One way that resistance shows up is in the narrowness of our short-term memory. We are exposed to billions of sensory inputs every second, but short-term memory only lets a few of those things into our conscious awareness, and even fewer into long-term memory storage. This is one way the brain maintains its integrity and maintains order in its storage area.

Another way is by requiring the items stored in long-term memory to be labeled for retrieval (via encoding) and stored in meaningful packages (schemas).[10] We've covered those ideas earlier.

The term *cognitive load* describes the difficulty involved in getting new information through the brain's narrow doorway so it can be stored in schemas for future retrieval.[11] If cognitive load is *high*, then learning is difficult.

What would make it hard to get a package filled with information through the brain's narrow doorway? Let's revisit our warehouse metaphor. There are three situations that could make it hard.

- The information inside the package might be very big or very heavy, making the package difficult to fit or carry through the narrow doorway.
- The package could be bulky or poorly designed so that it won't fit through the doorway even if the information inside the package, by itself, would fit.
- The workers trying to get the package through the doorway might be too bored, distracted, or lazy to get the package through the doorway and properly store and label its contents on the warehouse shelves.

Each of those situations is a metaphor for a different type of cognitive load, a different factor that could interfere with getting information out of your brain and into your learners' brains via your online course.

I'm going to teach you how to manage cognitive load in designing both your course as a whole, and your individual lessons and lesson materials. But first we have to delve deeper into the three different types of cognitive load. In order to manage cognitive load effectively, you first have to understand what it is and the various ways it can interfere with your course and lesson delivery.

Three Types of Cognitive Load

Researchers have identified three main types of cognitive load: intrinsic, extrinsic, and germane.[12] We are going to examine each type in turn with a view to understanding what it means for your course and lesson design.

Intrinsic Cognitive Load

Learning anything new has a certain amount of difficulty built into it. That's because when we learn something new, we are actually changing our brains. The difficulty that is an integral or built-in part of a subject matter is *intrinsic cognitive load*. (This would equate to a package whose contents are very large or very heavy, in our warehouse analogy.)

Let's face it, learning about nuclear physics, organic chemistry, or the mechanics of running a power plant is going to be hard. If it were easy, everyone would do it and we would all be rocket scientists.

So why can some people learn nuclear physics easily, while others can't? Well, for one thing, there is the factor of motivation. In order to overcome the challenges posed by high intrinsic cognitive load, you have to be highly motivated to learn the subject matter. A strong motivation will enable the learner to persist long enough and effectively enough to learn the material, even though the material is naturally difficult.

That motivation could be internal, such as if the student is passionate about the subject matter. Or it could be external, such as if the student must learn the subject matter in order to get a job, keep a job, advance in a job, avoid a penalty, or fulfill a legal or academic requirement. (If you are creating your online course independently, outside of a university or corporate setting, your learners probably don't have those types of external motivations, though.)

Another critical factor is the learner's prior knowledge. Prior knowledge is so important that universities impose prerequisites on certain subject matter. If you want to take a course in organic chemistry, you probably have to first take and pass courses in regular chemistry, basic biology, and so on. That's because the new schemas you are going to be building as you learn the concepts in the organic chemistry course, require you to have other schemas already present and functioning in your long-term memory that relate to the basic concepts of the course.

It is important to get some sense of what your students know before you create your course, in order to design the course effectively. If it turns out that your learners don't have the prior knowledge they need, you could build the necessary prior knowledge into your course. Or you could create a prerequisite course that they have to take first.

So, what does this mean for you, as a course creator? Even though a subject may be inherently difficult (it may have high intrinsic cognitive load), you can design your course in ways that make it easier for your students to access the material. You do that by:

- Breaking the material up into small chunks.
- Teaching one chunk at a time.
- Designing your course in ways that allow learners to process each chunk thoroughly.
- Building on the learner's prior knowledge.
- Not adding any unnecessary (extraneous) cognitive load.

Extraneous Cognitive Load

Extraneous cognitive load is information that is not a built-in part of the subject matter. For example, let's say someone is trying to teach you how to make a sandwich. The subject matter is not complicated. But if the explanation is complex or unclear it burdens the brain of the student. In the warehouse analogy, this would equate to a bulky or poorly designed package.

A subject like nuclear physics is hard in and of itself, but we don't have make it harder to learn through poor course or lesson design. We don't have to add extraneous cognitive load. Unclear explanations, irrelevant diversions, and other roadblocks to learning add extraneous cognitive load to any type of subject matter.

You can greatly improve your student's learning experience by minimizing (or better yet, completely eliminating) extraneous cognitive load. The online learning environment itself adds extraneous cognitive load to any type of subject matter, as compared to the in-person learning environment. But the course and lesson design techniques I'll be teaching you later in this book will show you how to minimize that extraneous cognitive load as much as possible.

Germane Cognitive Load

Germane cognitive load is a measurement of the intensity of engagement in mental work required to process new information for inclusion in long-term memory. A less technical way of saying that is: no pain, no gain. In order for learners to effectively build new mental muscles, they must be actively engaged in mental work.[13] Germane cognitive load measures the intensity of the mental workout you have created for your students, to help them actively interact with the new material and build new schemas around it.

In the warehouse analogy, you (as a course designer) would be trying to keep the workers (students) motivated. You do that by building a carefully calibrated amount of engagement into your learning activities. Your online lessons need to keep learners focused, interactive, and alert, so they don't get too bored, distracted, or lazy to move and store the new material you're presenting them with.

This is where the real art and science of teaching comes in, especially online.

Some things that seem like they should work online (like making things easy and simple for learners), don't always work. For example, it's important to make things easy for students by reducing extraneous cognitive load. But if you just hand things to students on a platter or serve up rote answers you want them to parrot back, your learners won't experience the levels of challenge and sustained involvement needed to build mental schemas on their own. There won't be enough germane cognitive load to keep them engaged in the learning task.

It's not enough just to hand students your own schemas. They have to build their own. Building a mental schema takes work. Our job as online course creators is to design learning experiences that guide students through the steps they need to follow to build their own schemas.

Being passionate about your subject matter is *why* you are the teacher. But your job is to ensure that your *students* know the subject matter. Making that happen effectively is *how* you are the teacher.

Germane cognitive load is a measure of the effective mental work your students must do in order to build a new mental schema or add to their existing schemas, to hold the information in your lesson in long-term memory. If germane cognitive load is too low and students are not required to do any mental work, they can end up feeling passive and disengaged from the learning task. If you are handing them stuff on a platter and they are simply regurgitating it back, they may pass an exam or meet some requirement, but no real long-term learning is taking place.

If germane cognitive load is too high, you may have designed a fascinating and engaging activity or game that ironically distracts your course participants from learning the material. If all of the learner's attention is focused on the activity, the actual subject matter of your course may get lost. Students will remember that they played a fun game or enjoyed an interactive activity, but not remember what you actually wanted them to learn.

So how much germane cognitive load is enough? You want to make the lesson material engaging and interactive enough to help the learner build an accurate mental schema to store the information you are teaching them. Once the game or activity or learning tool you've designed has achieved that, it has done what it needs to do.

The challenge in managing cognitive load is to maintain the delicate balance needed to nudge learners out of their comfort zone without overwhelming the limits of their short-term memory. You can lose the learner in more than one direction: into boredom, into overwhelm, or into over-involvement with an activity that is not essential to learning.

In a physical classroom, teachers receive ample feedback that lets them know how their students are handling this clutch point. Face-to-face teachers can see if the whole class or an individual student is lost, confused, or bored. It's harder for online teachers to get this type of feedback, but it's not impossible.

As an online teacher, feedback needs to be an integral part of your lesson design, so you have a way to quickly see if your students are engaged and learning, bored and wandering, or overwhelmed and lost.

Managing Cognitive Load in Online Learning

Cognitive load is a moving target that requires constant management. This is especially true if you are transferring a course or presentation from one context to another, such as from a face-to-face setting to an online setting. The affordances and constraints of the online-learning space change the cognitive load balance in various ways. That's why you can't just turn a classroom-based presentation into an online course by digitizing it. You have to redesign the presentation specifically for the online space, if you want it to work well there. (The good news is, I'm going to show you how to do that in a way that is fast, easy, and fun).

Cognitive load theory explains why attempts to transfer classroom-based programs online by simply digitizing existing content fall flat. Watching a video of a live presentation does not have the same level of germane cognitive load as attending the same presentation in person. When you attend in person, you can interact with the people around you, ask the instructor questions directly, and experience sensory inputs related to being there physically in real time. When you watch a video of the same presentation, you can't relate in as many sensory and social ways. You can still access the information, but several layers of engagement are missing.

So how do you build those layers of engagement into your online course? We'll be exploring that question and answering it throughout the remainder of this book.

Help Learners Process Information Using Lower- and Higher-Order Thinking Skills

Bloom's taxonomy classifies and organizes learners' ways of processing information from the most basic ways to the most advanced.[14] The taxonomy organizes thinking skills into two major groups: lower-order and higher-order thinking skills. There have been further elaborations of Bloom's taxonomy that integrate it with online learning tools, activities, and media.[15]

Lower-order thinking skills include remembering, understanding, and applying what was learned. Many lessons, both on and offline, don't go beyond that point. But to truly engage the learner and make sure the subject matter has been permanently stored in long-term memory, it's important also to include higher-order thinking skills.

Higher-order thinking skills include analyzing new information, evaluating it (or using it to evaluate other things), and finally, creating something new that demonstrates the learning that has taken place.

We'll return to these ideas after we talk about how to set up your course and plan your lessons.

Let's Review What We've Covered So Far

We've explored the difference between simply exposing people to information and actually teaching them; and we've discussed how teaching requires arranging a series of events that promote learning.

In order to understand what learning involves, we've talked about the limited capacity of working memory to hold information, so that only a few things can get through the brain's narrow "doorway" at any given time. We've also talked about how learners need to process the information they take in and store it in long-term memory in ways that are meaningful to them. In addition, we've discovered that learning requires us to create mental structures, schemas, to hold new information in long-term memory.

We've looked at what cognitive load theory tells us about the things that make learning difficult: material that is too hard, teaching that is poorly designed, and engagement that is too low.

We've considered what you can and can't do in the online-learning space, especially compared to the face-to-face learning space. Some things do not work to create effective and engaging online learning. Long talking-head videos, for example, overwhelm the learner's working memory and provide an underwhelming amount of engagement with the subject matter. Trying to put effective classroom-based learning online by simply digitizing it doesn't work because the results are not as engaging as the classroom-based version.

In Part Two, we're going to consider what *does* work to create effective and engaging online learning.

PART TWO

THE COURSE DESIGN
FORMULA®

....

FOUR

HOW THE FORMULA WORKS: AN OVERVIEW

My unique course design process, the Course Design Formula®, helps you design your course based on research into how people best learn the exact type of material you want to teach.

The Course Design Formula® will give you a competitive edge in creating your online course (or a complete membership site) by ensuring that your course truly *delivers* the transformation it promises. In developing this formula, I synthesized best practices from cognitive psychology, instructional design, learning theory, information processing theory, and more. The formula is based on my:

- Forty years of teaching and instructional design training and experience.

- Two master's degrees in education, one of which is a master's in instructional technology.
- Public education programs I created and ran for fifteen years that reached over 150,000 people and won regional and national awards.
- Certificate of completion in online teaching.
- Twelve years of research into how to translate classroom based teaching to online.
- Work with experts creating courses of many different types.

While the formula is based on instructional design principles that are known to course creators working in university and corporate training settings, I am making this expertise available to you as an independent online course creator in a way that is fast, fun, effective, and simple to apply to your specific content and target audience. If your goal is not just to sell a digital product, but to become a world-changing global teacher, the Course Design Formula® will help you get there. You will build your course better, faster, and more effectively than others who are not using a research-based instructional design process.

How the Formula Works: An Overview

Your course has different levels:

- The whole-course level
- The module level
- The lesson level
- The content level

In designing and building your course, it is best to start from the top (the whole-course level) and work your way down. Selecting the media to share your lesson content will be one of the last steps you take in building your course, after your instructional design decisions have been made. The reason for doing this is that your course's media artifacts should be the *result* of a planned learning process, not the cause.

The factors that determine how you build your course must be the requirements of human learning, not the requirements of your media or course platform.

Before You Begin: Understand the Different Levels of Your Course

Let's use the metaphor of building a house as a way to conceptualize the building of an online course. That metaphor will help us develop schemas that allow us to think about how the different levels of a course relate to each other and to the course as a whole.

Why is it important to be aware of the different levels within your course and how they relate to each other? It's important because, as you design and build your course, you will focus on these different levels at different times.

This approach is radically different from the way most people go about designing a course. The method most people use, which is the natural and intuitive (but largely ineffective) way, is to start at the beginning by creating lesson content using digital media and work forward step by step in increments. The problem with that method is that if any of those steps are calibrated wrong, the design gets farther and farther off track, until the whole course ends up at a different destination than the one you intended. At that point, you may have to discard media items you worked hard to create, which you later realize don't actually belong in your finished course.

To save you time and effort and be sure your course ends up at the destination you intended, we will instead organize it from the end first and the top down. The name for this type of design process is *backward design*.[1] You might find it familiar from Stephen R. Covey's reminder, in *The 7 Habits of Highly Successful People*, to "begin with the end in mind."[2]

We will start by considering the course as a whole and understanding the exact type of learning it contains. That specific type of learning will be used to create a general shape or container for the information you'll be sharing with your course participants. That shape or container will be based on Gagné's research into how people learn specific types of material, best.[3]

Gagné divided learning into five different areas or *domains,* which we will be talking about next.[4] Any of those types of learning can apply to your course at the course level, the module level, the lesson level, and the content level.

Imagine that your course as a whole is shaped like a triangle. If it were a house, the whole house could be shaped like a triangle (or, since a house is a 3D structure, like a pyramid).

Within a house, there are different levels or floors. Each level or floor within the house represents a module or chapter or large section within your course. A house has different levels to provide stability and structure that create space for the rooms where the actual living goes on. In our metaphor, your course has modules to create space for the lessons where the actual learning goes on. In the imaginary example we're using, the house as a whole has a triangular/pyramid shape, but each of the floors may have a different shape. One floor might be a rectangle, another a square, and so on.

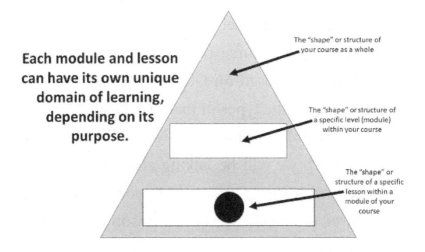

Figure 4.1. The structure of your course as a whole, your modules, and your lessons can all be different from each other. (Source: Learn and Get Smarter, Inc.)

In a house, each room has its own function. Different things go inside a kitchen than a living room, and the design of each room reflects its unique purpose. The same is true of the lessons in your course. Each lesson in each module of your course can have its own unique domain of learning, depending on its purpose.

Once we have set up the shape of the whole house, and of each floor within the house, and of each room on each floor within the house, then it is time to pick out the décor and furniture that make a house a home. To continue our extended metaphor, once we have determined the shape of your course as a whole (based on the specific type of transformation you want your course to deliver), set up the modules, and laid out the lessons, then it will be time to select the media that make the course something people can learn from.

Notice how different this process is from the way most people begin to design an online course. What most people instinctively do is start by selecting media (generally video or PDF) and creating content. The problem with doing that without first using the design process I'm sharing here, is that you can end up with the equivalent of a lone couch sitting by itself out in the woods. The media in your course should be the result, not the cause, of your design plan for how people will learn what you're trying to teach them. Any media decisions you make need to fit correctly into the larger picture of the transformation your course promises to deliver.

If you were building a house, you would start with a blueprint for the house as a whole, and you would start by laying a solid foundation. No matter how excited you are about picking out wallpaper and furniture, you would wait to do that until you had a solid foundation, well-framed walls, level floors, and rooms with actual walls.

You would design the house first, then create the levels of the house, then put the rooms into the levels, then pick out your décor. That way, you would end up with a coherent, well-designed, solid house that people could actually live in.

We will use a similar process to design your course.

The critical first step, which makes everything else fall into place, is to start at the whole-course level by determining the exact transformation you want your course to deliver.

The specific type of transformation you want your course to deliver will be one of five possible types, which relate to Gagné's five domains of learning. We'll go into the domains of learning later in depth, but if you're eager for a sneak peek, they are:

- Verbal information.
- Attitudes.
- Cognitive strategies.
- Intellectual skills.
- Motor skills.

Now let's continue on with our house metaphor as we explore the various levels of your course. The specific domain of learning your course falls into will determine the shape of the course as a whole.

Once we know that, we will set up your modules. With the modules set up, it will then be fast and easy to lay out the lessons within each module. Then we will use what Gagné discovered about the steps needed to help people take in, process and store new information, to plan each lesson in your course.

Once you have your lessons planned, you will select the ideal media to get the point of each lesson across. A huge benefit of following this process in this order is that your media decisions will not be made arbitrarily, but rather will be based on the purpose of each lesson and on how learners can access and absorb the lesson's content most effectively.

As you design the actual learning items inside your course, I will encourage you to think ahead about how those items can be used in various ways. For example, if you teach a process that has multiple steps, and some of the steps are going to be part of more than one lesson that you teach in more than one course, you can plan ahead by creating your content in the form of reusable learning objects.[5] That way, you only need to make your introductory video about proper yoga breathing techniques (for example) once, and then you can use it across all your courses.

....

FIVE

STEP 1: GET CLEAR ON THE TRANSFORMATION YOUR COURSE DELIVERS

The purpose of an online course is to deliver a specific transformation. People buy courses so they can achieve a specific result that improves their lives. But interestingly, many experts who are creating online courses don't think about the transformation their courses deliver. They are focused on sharing their expertise and describing what they have achieved. In doing so, they are missing the point, which is to help course participants achieve transformations of their own.

The first thing you need to do in order to be sure your course delivers the transformation you promise, is to be very clear on what that transformation is. Everything you'll do to design your course depends on getting the answer to this one question right. Ask yourself: What will my course participants be able to do after completing my course that they can't do now?

It can be harder than it seems to answer that question. If you'd like some structured guidance to help you brainstorm your answer, I've created a free course-planning journal you can access on my website (see "Next Steps").

·······································

SIX

STEP 2: DISCOVER THE SPECIFIC TYPE OF LEARNING YOUR COURSE CONTAINS

This next step is where the magic begins. Once you are very clear on what your learners will be able to do as a result of taking your course, it's time to discover the exact type of learning required to get them there. I've created a quiz you can take to discover this, "What Do You Want to Teach?" which is available on my website (see "Next Steps").

Your quiz result will tell you the type of learning for your course as a whole.

Here's How to Understand the Different Learning Types

As we've been discussing, Gagné's research divides all learning up into five major types, the *five domains of learning.*[1] You will save considerable time and energy by structuring your course in the way that works best to help people learn in each learning domain. These course structures are like prebuilt schemas that you can use to transfer large amounts of complex information from your mind to your learners' minds. My work with experts designing all types of online courses confirms that these structures work to set up an online course on any topic quickly.

The five domains of learning (verbal information, attitudes, cognitive strategies, intellectual skills, and motor skills) apply to learning at any scale, from a whole course or even a whole group of courses in a membership site, down to a small portion of a single PDF or video.[2] No matter the scale, the same procedures work.

Let's begin by exploring the domain of verbal information.

Verbal Information

Verbal information refers to things you can state verbally. Examples include being able to:

- State your name and address.
- List the days of the week.
- Describe something that happened.

- Recite a poem or prose passage from memory.
- Summarize a passage from a book.
- Explain the effects that one thing has on something else.
- Compare and contrast the ideas of multiple theorists.

As the above examples show, verbal information can range from the very simple to the very complex.

What makes something "verbal information" is that the learner can demonstrate that they have learned it by making a verbal statement or declaration. In the case of simple lists, vocabulary, and memorization, learners can demonstrate their learning by stating the words exactly as they were learned.

In the case of more complex ideas, the verbal statement a learner makes does not need to be word for word. Rather it will be a statement that demonstrates that the learner has grasped the main ideas and important details of the subject matter and can formulate them in his or her own words.

"But wait," you might say, "doesn't that describe all learning?"

Well, does it?

For example, if I tell you, "I have learned how to do a cartwheel," does my statement demonstrate that I have learned it? You may trust me, believe me, and be willing to take my word for it, but the fact remains that I have not demonstrated my learning of it. You'd be most likely to say, "Show me."

Figure 6.1. Person doing a cartwheel. (Source: Getty Images)

That's because doing a cartwheel is a motor skill, and the only way I can demonstrate that I have learned a motor skill is by actually performing the movements correctly. I can only demonstrate that I've learned a motor skill by using my muscles, not by speaking words.

But if I tell you that I have memorized the Declaration of Independence, I can demonstrate that I have learned it by reciting it: *"When in the Course of human events it becomes necessary . . ."* This is why memorizing the Declaration of Independence falls into the domain of verbal information, while learning how to do a cartwheel does not.

What is the best way to teach verbal information?

Let's start off by pointing out the worst way, which is to throw a giant block of uninterrupted text, an hour of nonstop audio narration, or a long video of someone speaking to the camera in "talking head" format, at your learner, and hope it sticks.

The long wordy letters that I sent as a youth group leader before figuring out a better way, were examples of the what-not-to-do-when-presenting-verbal-information category.

Why are long blocks of undifferentiated, uninterrupted text or voice narration not helpful for teaching verbal information? After all, verbal information consists of words, so wouldn't presenting more words be better for teaching more verbal information?

Keeping in mind what we've explored previously about how people learn, I bet you can guess the problems.

Long blocks of text:

- Overwhelm the learner's short-term memory.
- Do not help learners relate new learning to what they already know.
- Do not help learners build new mental structures for storing new information in long-term memory.
- Destroy learner motivation because they are boring, overwhelming, and hard to remember.

- Do nothing to help learners identify and focus on the specific things they need to learn.

In other words, throwing large, undifferentiated pages of text (or long segments of audio or video) at your learners will expose them to verbal information, but won't help them learn it. That's like inviting someone over for a steak dinner, and then presenting them with a whole live cow (rather than a cooked, finished meal) when they get to your house.

The vegan analogy would be inviting someone over for tofu and presenting them with a field of unharvested soybeans.

If you want to help your learners learn verbal information, you have to help them *process* and *digest* it, step by step. It is important to break verbal information down into manageable chunks, present those chunks in the right order, and help learners relate the new information to their prior knowledge and already-built mental structures (schemas).[3]

Use of images, mnemonic devices, keywords, and relevant explanations can help learners process and remember verbal information better.

Here's another metaphor. If you think of the verbal information you want to present as a (metaphorical)

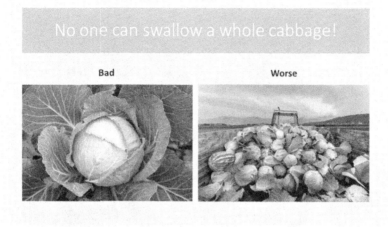

Figure 6.2. No one can swallow an entire cabbage—let alone a truckload! (Source: Learn and Get Smarter, Inc./ Getty Images)

cabbage, then teaching verbal information is like making cabbage salad. No one can eat a whole unprocessed cabbage in one sitting, let alone a truck load of cabbages.

But a finely sliced cabbage salad (properly "seasoned" with relevant graphics to provide context) is just right.

Why do these strategies work to teach verbal information? In the list of bullet points above, a consistently repeating format is used to present verbal information. Using a consistent format helps reduce extraneous cognitive load because the learner can anticipate what to expect with the presentation of each new piece of verbal information. Relevant images

Figure 6.3. Slice up your verbal information into tiny slivers. Serve it in an appropriate setting (context) and "season" with relevant graphics to promote learning. (Source: Getty Images)

provide an immediate and strong connection focused directly on the subject matter.

Even if your course as a whole does not teach verbal information, it's likely that various parts of it (modules, lessons, or learning objects) will.

Once you have your course structure set up, you will be able to identify which parts of it teach verbal information. Then you can chunk the verbal information into meaningful and memorable segments, accompanied by relevant graphics.

You can build features into your course content that provide a context for the verbal information, so that learners can relate it to what they already know. You can use imagery, mnemonics, and organizers in ways that will help the verbal information get into your learners' minds and stay there. (I'm guessing you remember that cabbage salad, right?)

You can build in features that ensure your learners will continue to use and apply the verbal information you're teaching, not only while taking your course but also in their lives going forward.

That's what it takes to transform a giant chunk of text or audio (the whole cabbage) into a digestible piece of instructional content (a tasty cabbage salad).

Cognitive Strategies

Cognitive strategies are methods for learning how to learn.

Courses that teach students how to prepare for tests, like the SAT, GRE, LSAT, and MCAT, teach cognitive strategies: ways to approach both the study leading up to the test, and the actual test questions themselves, in order to maximize success on the exam.

But cognitive strategies don't have to be about academic learning. A course that teaches how to know what someone really means by studying their body language, teaches a cognitive strategy. So does a course about learning the right type of dog for your family to buy, discovering the best fashion palette for your skin tone, or determining the right career choice for your personality type. A course that teaches *any kind of learning technique* falls into this domain of learning.

Gagné points out that cognitive strategies can help us learn how to do one particular thing, or can have broad applicability to all kinds of learning.[4]

Narrowly focused learning strategies are easiest to teach. Cognitive strategies that apply to a wide variety of situations take longer to teach, because learners need to practice applying the strategy under varying conditions to many types of material.[5] It is easier to learn a strategy for memorizing the days of the week in a foreign language using a mnemonic than to learn how to master any foreign language quickly, for example.

There are three phases to learning a cognitive strategy: understanding the strategy, practicing it, and observing its effectiveness. For the first part (understanding it), learners can be exposed to the cognitive strategy using verbal information, following the rules for presenting verbal information that we just went over.

For the second part (practicing it), learners need to actually practice the cognitive strategy in order to really learn it. Here you can see why it is easier to teach cognitive strategies that apply to very specific tasks, than those that apply to learning in general. Learners can easily practice a strategy that applies to a specific task, using that exact task. Once they have mastered it, they are done. They have learned the cognitive strategy.

But for cognitive strategies that apply across the board, such as learning how to break any complex problem down into its component parts, learners may need to practice the strategy on many different types of complex problems before they have fully mastered it.

Gagné points out that in such cases, the broader type of cognitive strategies (which he calls *executive strategies*) are developed over a long period of time, rather than learned quickly all at once, like the more specific type (which he calls *task strategies*).[6]

You may want to include a module or lesson near the beginning of your course that directs your students to the most effective way to approach and learn from your course as a whole. That section of your course will be teaching the cognitive strategy learners should use to get the most out of your course material. Since your course is specific rather than general, students will be able to master the cognitive strategy needed to do well in your course quickly.

It will be helpful to present the cognitive strategy in three steps, as follows.

- **Step 1.** Explain the strategy directly using verbal information.
- **Step 2.** Provide an opportunity to practice the strategy using a short sample of your actual course material.
- **Step 3.** Provide learners with feedback on how well their use of the strategy worked for actually learning the material.

Your course might also include a section on cognitive strategies for mastering the actual subject your course is teaching. For example, if your course is about "how to improve your tennis swing," a motor skill, you might include a section on the "best way to approach mastering your swing" that could include cognitive strategies, such as reviewing videos of great tennis players, having a friend videotape your swing and then watching the video in stop motion to measure angles at various points, and so on. In this case, your instruction would include three parts as mentioned above. Provide:

- Information about what to do, using verbal information techniques.
- Ways for your student to practice the cognitive strategy.
- Feedback to your students on how well they are doing at implementing the strategy.

Later in this book, we will discuss how you can provide feedback to your students to show them if they have learned the material in your course. Providing feedback immediately after the practice session or activity will give students the confidence to know they are ready to proceed with your course and truly get the most out of it.

Attitudes

Either your course as a whole, or some section of it, may involve teaching attitudes. Having the right attitude is critical to success in many areas of life, ranging from personal motivation and workplace culture to competitive performance. Because attitudes are so important to success, many online learning programs focus on teaching them.

Examples of the types of courses that teach attitudes include topics such as:

- Develop your success mindset.
- Learn to love your body just as it is.
- Get over your breakup and learn to love again.
- Develop laser focus to dominate your market.
- Find the fun and joy in being home with your toddler all day.
- Overcome math phobia.
- Mental conditioning for athletes.
- Develop the motivation to quit smoking now.
- Just say no to drugs and alcohol.
- Learn to overcome procrastination and be more productive.
- Get out from under stress and overwhelm.

Gagné points out that teaching attitudes differs from teaching other kinds of material, because attitudes have more to do with feelings and behavior than with intellectually based information.7

It's not as easy to teach attitudes as it is to teach verbal information. Learners can't demonstrate to you (and sometimes themselves) that their attitude has changed by saying "I'm motivated now" or "I will quit smoking tomorrow." Attitudes can take a long time to learn and develop, and they can't be observed directly. Instead, you have to observe a learner's behavior over a long period of time in order to be sure that the desired attitude has been learned.[8] (Depending on the nature and context of your course, the learners' judgment on their learning outcomes may substitute for the instructor's. We'll discuss that at greater length later in this book).

For example, while saying "I will quit smoking tomorrow" signals an intention, and is a good place to start, it does not prove that the learner's attitude toward smoking has changed (from a good thing to a bad thing, or from something the student chooses to do to something the student chooses not to do). But if the learner is able to go for an extended period of time without smoking, that person's long-term nonsmoking behavior would be a good indication that his or her attitude toward smoking had changed.

If your online course as a whole, or a portion of it, focuses on changing the learner's attitude about something, what is the best way to go about teaching that?

First, let's be clear on what does not work: simply telling people to change their attitude.[9] (But then, if you're a parent, teacher, or coach, you already know that—am I right?)

However, attitudes *can* be taught or changed using both direct and indirect methods.[10] *Direct methods* include making learners aware of different types of attitudes they can have and apply under various conditions, and the pros and cons associated with each one. *Indirect methods* include role modeling, simulations, and role playing.[11]

Figure 6.4. If this young man told you, verbally, that he has changed his attitude about eating broccoli, would you believe him? (Source: Getty Images)

What does this mean in practical terms, for you, as an online course designer?

While it has not been found effective to directly say "Smoking is bad for you so cut it out right now!" you could instead point out (or better yet, clearly demonstrate) the health costs of smoking over the course of a lifetime, and the health benefits that come from not smoking.

This approach had a profound effect on my own life. When I was in the seventh grade, I saw an exhibit showing an actual human lung that had belonged to a lifelong smoker, on display at the American Museum of Natural History in New York City. The lung was completely charred and black; it looked like a lung-shaped piece of charcoal. That was all I needed to see to understand that I should never start smoking cigarettes if I did not want my own lungs to end up looking like that. Seeing that charred lung at a young age shaped my attitude toward smoking forever.

No one ever told me "Don't smoke, it's bad for you!" (As we've discussed above, that approach does not work well, especially with teenagers). But directly seeing the long-term effects of smoking on the human body was enough to immediately and permanently push my attitude toward smoking in the right direction.

As I understand it, a key factor in choosing to adopt a new attitude is indeed that it is a *choice*: the learner's *own* choice.

Attitudes that are forced on a learner are not really learned; they are simply imitated or faked (as any parent who has ever said "Tell your brother you're sorry!" can confirm).

The art in teaching attitudes consists in helping learners become aware of the attitude you want them to adopt, helping them understand the long-term benefits that adopting the new attitude holds for them, and helping them experience positive effects over time as they choose to adopt that new attitude.

Figure 6.5. Now his attitude toward eating broccoli has changed! (Source: Getty Images).

It is important that learners have a chance to practice adopting the new attitude, and experience its positive effects, until it becomes a habit for them. Otherwise, as with other types of learning, they won't have really learned the new attitude (and changed their brains to incorporate it) and will simply have been exposed to information about it.

The process of teaching attitudes, as I analyze and understand it, breaks down into the following major steps.

Step 1: Identify and explain the possible attitude options, along with their costs and benefits. The first step in designing instruction about attitudes is to make learners aware of the various types of attitudes they can choose to have, and the long-term costs and benefits of each option. For example, in programs designed to help people learn to forgive painful things that were done to them, the cost of not forgiving is often brought up.

These costs and benefits can be shared in the form of verbal information and can also be demonstrated using simulations and role playing that show the various alternative attitudes and how their effects pan out over time.[12]

Step 2: From this menu of options, identify and demonstrate the desired attitude choice. Once you have made your learners aware of the different types of attitudes they can choose to adopt, and the costs and benefits of each, it is important to model for them what the right option (the attitude you are trying to teach them) looks like.

Learners are more likely to copy the modeled attitude if it is demonstrated by a popular, well-known, and well-liked person that they identify with and look up to. This is one of the reasons that popular sports heroes are often featured in ads designed to modify attitudes toward specific products.[13] Cartoon figures and mascots that promote a particular point of view also serve this role-modeling purpose.

My own reflection is that the prevalence of popular figures online and in social media is a double-edged sword when it comes to teaching attitudes. Learners today are exposed to influences from many sources, including some featuring popular figures modeling attitudes and behaviors that we may not want learners to adopt. This fact highlights the importance of the next step for teaching attitudes.

Step 3: Model, reinforce, and reward the desired behavior. There are several factors that contribute to reinforcing the desired behavior (the behavior that results from the learner adopting the target attitude). One such factor is the environment. It would be very difficult to promote attitudes relating to adopting a healthy lifestyle in an environment filled with junk food and sugary treats that are placed everywhere at eye level, for example.[14]

For you, as an online course designer, an important aspect of teaching a course about adopting healthy eating habits would include helping your students modify their own environments to reward them for making healthy food choices. For example, you could encourage them to remove junk food from their fridge and cupboards, plan healthy and enjoyable treats for themselves, stay out of stores that sell lots of sugary snacks, and so on.

It is important to be sure that your own behavior as an educator reinforces and rewards your learners for adopting the attitude you are trying to teach. For example, if you have a section in your course that encourages students to adopt an attitude of diligence and turn in their assignments early, it's important that you provide timely feedback to those students who do turn in their assignments early, rather than making them wait until the other students have turned theirs in—otherwise, what is the benefit of turning work in early?

Make sure that your students have the skills they need to follow through on behaviors that reflect the attitude you are teaching them. If you are teaching about adopting a health-conscious attitude toward eating, make sure your students know which foods are and aren't health-promoting. If you are teaching a course about showing respect in the workplace by dressing appropriately, be sure to spell out what is meant, in that particular workplace, by the phrase *appropriate workplace attire.*

There is an intrinsic sense of reward that comes from doing what is expected and doing it well, but learners can only experience that sense of reward if they understand what is expected and what "doing it well" looks like.

Step 4: Keep the big picture in mind. To really teach an attitude, so that learners change their brains and modify their behavior, is a big responsibility. This is the kind of teaching that can truly make a difference in someone's life.

As with my smoking example, learning the right attitudes can actually save someone's life by helping them avoid behaviors that promote disease or dangerous risk-taking. With the right attitudes, learners can improve their health, their productivity, their performance, their income, their relationships, their emotional outlook and many other aspects of their lives.

The key to making that kind of positive change happen is that you have to actually *teach* the attitude in ways that ensure your students actually *learn* it. As with the other domains of learning, just talking *about* the desired attitude is not enough.

Some big-picture factors to keep in mind when teaching attitudes include linking the attitude to a larger set of values that are important to the learner.[15] One way to do this in an online course is to have the student reflect on their personal reasons for wanting to adopt the new mindset (perhaps in writing or by sharing in a forum or mastermind group).

Personal reasons for learning new attitudes are critical because without strong motivation, learners may just end up paying lip service to the new attitude as something that "sounds good," without really making it an integral part of their lives.

Any time we try to make real change in our lives, it is natural to encounter resistance, both from within ourselves and from our environment. Sometimes we end up taking three steps forward and two steps back. Really learning a new attitude and making it an ongoing part of our lives, as demonstrated through changed behavior, takes time and requires ongoing support.[16]

One way to provide support for attitude learning is to set up a sequence of lessons where you consistently help the learner practice and reinforce the target attitude and its resulting behaviors, including support and guidance for dealing with any slipups or setbacks that arise along the way. Another way is to provide an online community that promotes and reinforces the desired attitude change and its resulting behaviors. The fact that attitude change requires ongoing long-term support makes a mindset course an excellent foundation for an online membership site.

Figure 6.6. Course Crafters Camp™ landing page screenshot (Source: Learn and Get Smarter, Inc./ Getty Images)

I've created an online community, Course Crafters Camp™ (see "Next Steps"), to provide a supportive community and environment for experts who have completed my Course Design Formula® course. The purpose of Course Crafters Camp™ is to provide continuous positive support in implementing the attitudes toward online course design that I teach in this book.

Feedback is an important part of this support process. Without feedback, you, as the instructor, will have no way to know if your learners are actually opening your emails and completing the lessons, or if they are struggling at some point. It's important to be aware of those kinds of issues so you can help your students deal with them.

Mastermind groups can provide peer support that reinforces all group members as they work to adopt the target attitude and its resulting behaviors.

Really learning a new attitude can be hard, especially for adults who have had more time than children to get set in their ways. Sometimes there is not a lot of support for the new attitude in the learner's home or external environment. This is another reason why ongoing support from a teacher or group leader, and peer support in an online community, can be helpful for learning new attitudes and practicing the desired target behaviors that flow from them.

In order to teach attitude change, it's important to:
- Identify the desired behavior.
- Demonstrate the desired behavior.
- Reward the desired behavior.
- Provide opportunities for learners to practice the desired behavior.[17]

Intellectual Skills

A lot of online courses teach learners how to do something. Examples would be how to:

- Beat the stock market.
- Lose weight and keep it off forever.
- Get your ex back.
- Raise polite children.
- Excel in online marketing.
- Create realistic 3D models using AutoCAD.

Another example of a how-to course would be this very book you are reading whose subtitle is *How to Teach Anything to Anyone Online.*

Gagné's term for the domain of learning that teaches learners how to do something specific is *intellectual skills.*[18]

You might wonder about the emphasis on intellect in teaching how-to skills. I mean, isn't this area of learning more focused on *doing* things, than on thinking about them?

Aha! That's just where it gets interesting. Because in order to do something, in the how-to sense, you first have to understand exactly what it is you are doing, what (or who) you are doing it to, and under what conditions you are doing it . . . in the intellectual sense.

Gagné's research found that in order to really be able to do something (as opposed to just being exposed to information about how to do it), certain very specific steps need to be followed, and these steps involve an increasingly complicated hierarchy of intellectual learnings.[19]

Let's look at this book that you are reading, for example. The goal of this book is to teach a how-to skill: how to teach anything to anyone online. In order to know how to do that, you first have to understand the big ideas and concepts relating to how people learn and what constitutes good teaching. For instance, you need to understand how learning and teaching are affected by the move to an online learning space. You need to understand what educational theory and research suggest about best practices for teaching different types of subject matter.

"How to teach anything to anyone online" is a complex intellectual skill with many component parts. It takes a lot of prior knowledge to perform this skill well. That's why this book provides information designed to give you the prior knowledge you need in order to make it easy for you to actually design not only the course you are working on now, but also any other course you may want to design in the future.

You will ultimately be performing a how-to task: designing an online course. But in order to be ready to do that, you first have to understand the ideas and concepts that go into designing an excellent online course. The skillful layering of these prerequisite concepts is how a course designer slices, dices, prepares, seasons, and "cooks" the ideas needed to make the information digestible for the learner.

Let's take a very simple example of a how-to skill that one might teach a toddler, in order to understand what is involved in teaching someone how to do something. For example, let's teach our imaginary toddler how to cross the street.

Teaching a toddler how to cross the street involves teaching a series of rules.

- Stop.
- Wait.
- Hold Mommy's or Daddy's hand.
- Look both ways.
- Make sure there is no traffic coming.
- Cross the street when the light is green.

That seems fairly simple, doesn't it?

The actual rule being taught is: cross the street when the light is green. In rule form, this reads as follows: "*If* the light is green, *then* cross the street."

Why can't we just tell our two-year-old that up front, and have done with it?

Here's why. Imagine that you are two years old, and you are not entirely clear on exactly what is meant by *green*. (A two-year-old recently informed me with great confidence that many objects, of various different colors, were "red.") In order to be able to "cross the street when the light is green," children first must understand what *green* is. They must be able to *discriminate* green from other colors.[20]

But wait, there's more. Even if the toddler understands what *green* is, the child also needs to understand what a traffic light is and how it works. Otherwise the child might stand at the corner forever, waiting for a black metal traffic light to magically turn green all over, which is not going to happen.

And while we are on the subject of traffic lights, we also need to be sure our toddler understands what *traffic* is. We need to be sure the child understands what *There is no traffic coming* means.

We even need to be sure the child understands what a *street* is.

And what *cross* means.

Suddenly, teaching a toddler to cross the street doesn't seem so simple after all, does it?

The issue here, as with all how-to learning, is that in order to learn how to apply the rule "Cross the street when the light is green," our learner needs to have some very specific prior knowledge.

What does this mean for us as educators in terms of teaching how-to skills? It means we have to start with the simplest parts of this puzzle and then work our way up in complexity. The simplest parts are what Gagné calls *discriminations*: things you can clearly point to and discriminate (tell apart) from other things. [21] Our toddler must be able to discriminate green from red, stopping from going, traffic from no traffic, and the street from the sidewalk, in order to be ready to learn how to cross the street when the light is green.

Next, our learner must understand the concepts related to the rule being learned.[22] In this case, the toddler must understand that a traffic light changes colors, and that cars stop and go based on these colors, and the toddler must understand the concept of crossing a street by moving from one sidewalk to the other.

Finally, once our learner has that prior knowledge, we can teach the rule: *If* the traffic light is green, *then* cross the street.[23]

There may also be exceptions to the rule which are important to learn. For example: If the traffic light is green, then cross the street, *unless* there are cars coming (or *unless* a grownup tells you not to, or *unless* there is a police officer there, and so on).

Now that we have explored this example, we have the prior knowledge we need to begin to learn how to teach intellectual skills.

Teaching intellectual skills involves four main steps.[24]

1. Teach the *discriminations* the learner needs to know in order to apply the rule.
2. Teach the *concepts* the learner needs to know in order to apply the rule.
3. Teach the *rule.*
4. Teach any *exceptions* to the rule.

Teaching discriminations is fairly easy. However, the place where one can get tripped up in teaching intellectual skills is at the level of concepts. One reason teaching concepts is hard is that we need to be very clear on what each concept is that we are trying to teach.

For example, for the intellectual skill that you are grappling with right now as you read this book, we're exploring how to teach anything to anyone online. We started by focusing on what teachers must be able to observe in order to know if their students are actually learning. Teachers must be able to tell (discriminate) whether their students are paying attention and understanding the instruction. But you *can't* directly observe that in your online course, due to the constraints of the online-learning space. So, we explored concepts relating to the affordances and constraints of online learning. Now we are up to the level of complex concepts you must understand in order to teach anything to anyone online. Those concepts include *cognitive load, lower- and higher-order thinking skills, the five domains of learning,* and so on.

Clearly, learning how to teach anything to anyone online is a much more complex how-to skill than teaching a toddler how to cross the street. One reason it is more complex is that it requires prior knowledge of complex concepts that need to be clearly defined.[25] Gagné tells us that when concepts are complex, the instructor must both identify and also define these concepts for the learner.[26]

When teaching how-to skills that depend on complex defined concepts, the instruction can easily run off the rails at this specific point. You, the instructor, must have a crystal-clear grasp of the concepts your learners need to know in order to apply the rule you are going to teach them. You must also define these concepts in ways that make them crystal clear to your learners. Failure to correctly complete this critical step will cause your instruction to fall apart from this point forward.

That might sound like big, bad, scary news, yet it's not. It's actually very helpful and encouraging news. Why? Because it means that if you are trying to teach a how-to skill and you run into trouble doing it, the first thing to do is go back and review the concepts that learners must understand in order to perform the skill. These are the concepts your rule is built on. So it's critical that you correctly define and clarify those concepts for your learners before trying to teach them how to perform the steps of the skill.

The good news is that once your learners have the prior knowledge they need, they should be able to learn the rule (the how-to skill) easily. If your learners fully understand the discriminations and concepts they need, then learning the rule itself should come easily.

If learning the rule does *not* come easily to your learners, go back and tighten up your defined concepts and try teaching the rule again.

Motor Skills

Motor skills are made up of two important components: movement and skill.

As I mentioned earlier, when talking about demonstrating that you've learned how to do a cartwheel, you can't demonstrate your ability just by saying it exists. The only way to demonstrate a cartwheel (or tango dancing, javelin tossing, and juggling) is actually to perform the movement in a skillful manner.[27]

Motor skills have some things in common with intellectual skills, because they include rules for how to do something: *if* you want the car to go left, *then* turn the steering wheel toward the left. But intellectually learning the rules for doing a movement is only the first step in learning a new motor skill.

It is only the first step because it's not enough for the learner simply to know the steps that make up the movement being taught. Learners must also have specific, direct, physical opportunities to practice those steps until they can perform them automatically as part of a smooth movement routine.[28] In order to actually learn a motor skill, learners must be able to perform it, skillfully, automatically, and with ease using their own bodies.

For example, let's say that a learner is taking his driver's license road test at the Department of Motor Vehicles. Imagine that the DMV examiner tells the student, "Turn left." Now imagine that the student sits there mumbling under his breath, "If I want to turn left, I have to turn the steering wheel to the left." Do you think this student would pass his road test?

No? Why not? I mean, he knew the correct action to take to make the car turn left, didn't he?

Yes, he knew it intellectually, but he wasn't able to perform the movement skillfully and automatically, without having to stop and think about it.

For motor skills, if you can't perform the action or sequence of actions skillfully and automatically without having to stop and think about it, you haven't yet learned the motor skill.

The reason for this is obvious: we can't have a road full of drivers sitting in cars reciting to themselves what the steps are for how to change lanes, how to speed up or slow down, and so on. The movements needed to drive skillfully must be automatic in order for a driver to be on the road safely.

As I sit here writing this book, my mind is engaged in thinking thoughts that take the form of words. At the same time, my fingers are flying over the keyboard, causing those words to appear on my computer screen as if by magic. But it's not magic, it's a motor skill known as *touch typing*.

When we first start to learn touch typing, we need to be taught where each letter is on the keyboard. But if we keep having to look for each letter one at a time, visually, we may get stuck at the hunt-and-peck stage. In order to really know touch typing, we have to be able to perform the movements effortlessly without looking at the keyboard or thinking about the movements at all.

The only way to learn any motor skill is to practice, practice, practice.

In terms of typing, the only way to learn is to practice the movements without looking at the keyboard. We have to know how far to move each finger in order to make it hit the key that produces each letter.

Teaching motor skills requires attention to three steps.

1. Teach the individual movements or steps that make up the motor skill.

2. Put these individual steps together into a smooth routine.

3. Provide opportunities for learners to practice the routine over and over until they can do it effortlessly without having to stop and think about it.

It is important for you as a course designer to ensure your learners will receive immediate feedback as they begin to practice putting the steps of the movement activity together and performing them as a routine.[29]

When teaching a motor skill, feedback should be *immediate*: provided as soon as the learner has performed the movement routine.

The feedback should also be specific, so that the learner knows exactly which aspects of the movement activity they did well and which aspects they still need to improve in order to reach an acceptable standard of performance.

Most importantly, learners need to know exactly what and how to improve. Here are some examples of specific feedback.

- "Turn the steering wheel a little more to the left next time."
- "The jump comes *after* the hop, not before it."

- "Lean forward a little more as you lift your other leg."

Teaching motor skills in an online context can present challenges, depending on the type of motor skill being taught. Some motor skills, such as touch typing, lend themselves well to online learning. For example, a touch-typing program for online learning can provide immediate feedback about which letters the learner typed incorrectly, how long the learner took to complete the typing sample, and so on.

An online touch-typing session also can be followed by immediate remedial practice on the letters that were missed. Students can practice touch typing in an online setting at any hour of the day or night and receive immediate feedback without the teacher having to be physically present to provide it, using software that is appropriately programmed to offer this type of feedback.

The nature of touch typing as a physical activity makes it easy to practice in an online setting. And practice is the most important factor in learning a motor skill.

Water skiing, on the other hand, would be challenging to teach online—at least, the part of water skiing that requires the learner to be physically immersed in a large body of water while being pulled by a boat at a high rate of speed.

If your goal is to teach motor skills and you are teaching online, it is important to be clear about the parts of the learning process you can and can't teach entirely online.

For all motor skills, it should be possible to explain the sequence of steps needed to perform the skill, using online methods. For example, if you do an online search for the phrase *"How to water ski"* you will find many websites using PDFs, videos, and other multimedia tools that describe waterskiing techniques.

But at some point, in order to really learn how to waterski, learners are going to have get into the water behind a fast boat. And if and when they do, it is going to be critically important that their water-based instructors first verify that learners have all the prior knowledge needed in order to learn how to water ski. In this case, important prior knowledge includes knowing how to swim, knowing how to hold onto the rope, knowing how to position the skis, knowing how to signal for help, knowing what to do if you fall over or lose hold of the rope, and more.

While you can learn some preparatory aspects of how to water ski online, you cannot actually practice the physical movements that together make up water skiing unless you physically get into the water, hold onto a water ski handle, and experience what it feels like to be pulled across a large flat surface of water by a very fast boat.

Much of the learning for motor skills, such as water skiing, ice skating, snow skiing, and performing industrial, surgical and dental procedures, comes from the learner's repeated experience in using his or her own muscles and joints to compensate for physical forces that may include gravity, friction, speed, pressure, wind, resistance, and so on.

There is no way (at least, not yet!) to provide the immersion part of some experiences in an online context. That is one of the constraints of online learning. What you can do as an online instructor, however, is bring technology out into the field, using apps such as Coach's Eye or GoPro (see "Resources"), which enable you to observe your learners' physical performance in real time, and provide immediate feedback to them online.[30]

Virtual reality simulators also play an important role in training athletes, physicians, and others to perform motor skills.

While it will ultimately be necessary for athletes to actually get out onto the playing field and doctors to step into the operating room, they will be more prepared to do so if they can learn the movement steps, practice, and train in advance—all of which *can* be done online.

While it is currently unlikely that individual online course creators will have access to complex and expensive virtual reality (VR) simulators for students to use, that could change in the future. The potential of VR simulation for motor-skills training is just beginning to be tapped.[31]

If your goal is to teach motor skills in an online context, then it will be interesting to keep up with the latest developments in VR simulations for online use in the next handful of years.[32] This field is currently in early stages of development, but the potential is there to make it easier for online course creators to design personalized immersive learning environments for their students' use. This would be especially useful for teaching motor skills.

Let's take an example of a motor skill that falls midway between touch typing and water skiing in terms of how easy it would be to teach online. Let's say that you want to teach salsa dancing. The online learning interface lends itself to teaching the terminology and basic dance steps that go into salsa dancing. You could also provide printed patterns of dancing feet in the various positions your students will need to hit as they perform the dance in real life.

You could instruct students to print out the feet patterns, cut them out, and place them on the floor in the proper locations (which you can demonstrate using a printable diagram or map). You could then create a video in which you model the dance steps, first in slow motion and then at normal speed. You then could ask your students to practice dancing to the same music you used in the example, placing their own feet on top of the cut-out patterns at appropriate times. You could instruct learners to have someone video them, and then compare their own video to the model you provided. It is particularly helpful when teaching motor skills to provide learners with an example of what correct performance looks like.[33]

To really solidify the learning, you could encourage your students to perform self-evaluations by writing down observations of how their salsa dancing performance differs from the model, and what they can do to make it come closer to the model the next time. Then have them practice again, video record again, and look for points of improvement as they watch the replay of their second performance. A helpful affordance of online learning for teaching motor skills is that your learners will have an ongoing, tangible record of their improvement step by step.

Another exciting feature of learning motor skills online is that they can be improved by mental practice.[34] Mental practice or rehearsal lends itself very well to the affordances of online teaching. For example, you could encourage mental practice of the motor skills you are teaching by providing a downloadable audio file that guides your students through the steps of the motor skill. That way your students can listen to the steps of the movement routine while they either physically practice or mentally visualize themselves performing the motions.

Intellectually learning the movement steps of the skill is a necessary first part of learning any motor skill. Being able to visualize and list the components of the motor skill is important, too. Mental practice by visualizing yourself going through the movements can be helpful. But it cannot be emphasized enough that the only way you can actually learn a motor skill—as opposed to just being exposed to information about it— is to physically practice the actual movements that make up the motor skill, over and over, in the actual physical world, using your actual physical body.

Depending on the motor skill being taught, it may not be possible to get students to the necessary level of automatic muscle memory performance through online teaching alone. I point this out here, so you won't be disappointed in case that happens. We do have to take the affordances and constraints of the online learning situation into consideration after all.

Even with the best simulations available, it is necessary to get behind the wheel of an actual car in order to learn how to drive, and it is necessary to get onto an actual bike in order to learn how to ride one.

Maybe someday VR technology will reach a level where we really can learn every motor skill in a completely virtual context. However, at least for independent course creators working on their own outside the context of organizations with large budgets, the technology available is simply not at that point yet.

But what about instruction that *does* have the benefit of large budgets and state-of-the-art simulations for teaching motor skills? One example is the medical field, where doctors learn to perform complex procedures using high-end customized simulation software. Certainly, such simulations play an important part in helping doctors to practice complex and unique sets of motor skills, especially for treatment of rare conditions and performing difficult surgeries where opportunities to practice under real conditions may be hard to find.

I am sure that all of us, as potential live patients, would prefer that our doctor has had ample practice using a simulation rather than no practice at all. But does practice using simulation lead to expert performance when working with real patients? This issue is of great importance from the perspective of both patient outcomes and institutional costs. Current research suggests that simulation-based training is important and helpful for learning motor skills although it cannot replace actual training with real patients in the real world.[35]

The situation with advanced simulation software is similar to the situation we face as independent course creators—technology-based learning has an important role to play in teaching motor skills, but true mastery requires actual practice in the real world.

SEVEN

....

STEP 3: SET UP YOUR MODULES TO SUPPORT YOUR COURSE'S LEARNING GOAL

We've explored Gagné's findings about the five domains of learning and talked about how he found people learn best in each domain. Now we will explore how to use these discoveries to structure your course.

Let's clarify the module structure for a course that falls into each learning domain. Here's how to set up your course modules based on the learning goal for your course as a whole.

For a Verbal Information Course

Setting up a verbal information course is like slicing a cabbage to make cabbage salad. (No one can eat a whole cabbage, but it's easy to swallow and digest tiny slivers of cabbage.) First make big cuts to divide your course/cabbage into chunks. Then make smaller cuts facing in either the same, or a different, direction, to slice the chunks into digestible slivers.

Figure 7.1: Dividing up the modules and lessons in a verbal information course is like slicing a cabbage. (Source: Learn and Get Smarter, Inc./Getty Images)

Use one method to divide the verbal information in your course as a whole into big chunks. For example, you can chunk your course modules by:

- Time periods.
- People.
- Types.
- Items.
- Features.
- Benefits.

- Systems, methods, or processes.
- Big ideas.

Then, use either the same method, or a different method to divide each module into smaller lesson chunks.

Here's an example of a verbal information course that uses one method to divide the modules into big chunks, and a different method to divide the lessons into smaller chunks. The modules are divided by *geographical region*. The lessons are divided by *types of orchids* found within each region.

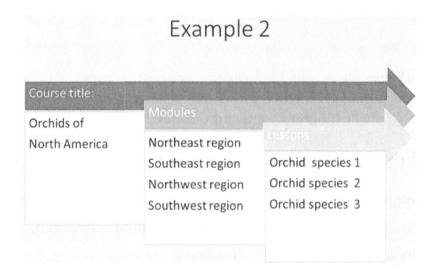

Example 2

Course title:	Modules	Lessons
Orchids of North America	Northeast region	
	Southeast region	Orchid species 1
	Northwest region	Orchid species 2
	Southwest region	Orchid species 3

Figure 7.2: A verbal information course that uses a different chunking method for its modules and its lessons. (Source: Learn and Get Smarter, Inc.)

Here's a second example of a verbal information course using the same method to divide the modules into big chunks and the lessons into smaller chunks. Both are divided by *time period.* The modules are divided by centuries and the lessons are divided by decades.

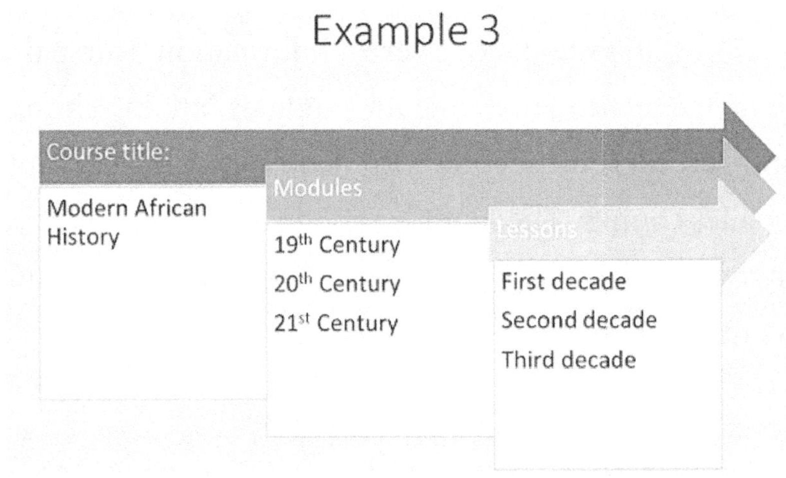

Example 3

Course title:
Modern African History

Modules
19th Century
20th Century
21st Century

Lessons
First decade
Second decade
Third decade

Figure 7.3: A verbal information course that uses the same chunking method for its modules and its lessons. (Source: Learn and Get Smarter, Inc.)

For an Attitudes/Mindset Course

For a course that teaches an attitude or mindset change, my suggestion, which is based on Gagné's research, is to set up your modules this way[1]:

- **Module 1:** Present the ineffective attitude choices the learner could make and the long-term results of making those ineffective choices.

- **Module 2**: Present the effective attitude choice that will work better in the long term.
- **Module 3**: Help learners identify positive role models who can demonstrate the benefits of adopting the effective attitude choice.
- **Module 4**: Help learners find their *"why"* (motivational reason) for adopting the effective attitude choice. They need to identify both a short-term "why" (to see immediate results) and a long-term "why" (for continuing motivation once short-term results are achieved).
- **Module 5**: Provide long-term, ongoing support. A mindset course works well as the foundation for a support community or membership site. That's because in order to achieve a lasting mindset change, learners need consistent positive reinforcement for adopting the target attitude, as well as the opportunity to observe and interact with positive role models.[2]

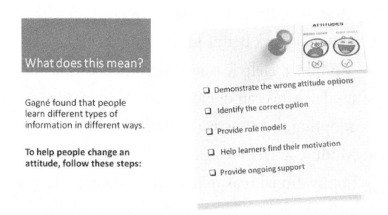

What does this mean?

Gagné found that people learn different types of information in different ways.

To help people change an attitude, follow these steps:

ATTITUDES

☐ Demonstrate the wrong attitude options

☐ Identify the correct option

☐ Provide role models

☐ Help learners find their motivation

☐ Provide ongoing support

Figure 7.4: How to set up the modules for a course that teaches an attitude or mindset change. (Source: Learn and Get Smarter, Inc./Getty Images)

For a Cognitive Strategies Course

Teach a cognitive strategy in three phases.

- **Phase 1.** Explain the strategy.
- **Phase 2.** Help learners practice the strategy.
- **Phase 3.** Help learners get feedback on how well they did.

You can structure your course by setting up a separate module for each of those steps. Or you can have modules that focus on different types of subject matter you want the learner to practice on and repeat those three steps as lessons within each module.

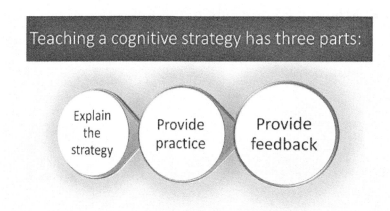

Figure 7.5: The three stages of teaching a cognitive strategy.
(Source: Learn and Get Smarter, Inc.)

For an Intellectual Skills/How-To Course

To set up an intellectual skills course that teaches a simple procedure or rule, think of how you would teach someone to bake a cake.

Here's how to set up the modules for a course that teaches a *simple* "how-to" skill.

- **Module 1:** Teach the basic things a learner must know/do/have to be able to perform the skill.
- **Module 2:** Teach the concepts or big ideas a learner must understand to be able to perform the skill.
- **Module 3:** Take the learner through the steps of performing the skill.

- **Module 4**: Point out any modifications, clarifications or exceptions to the rules you just taught.

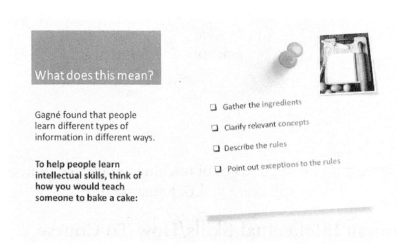

Figure 7.6. How to set up an intellectual skills (how-to) course. (Source: Learn and Get Smarter, Inc./Getty Images)

Here's a modification to the rule I just taught about how to set up an intellectual skills course: If the skill you are teaching is complex, in actual practice it often works best to reverse the order of modules 1 and 2. For a *complex* intellectual skills course, set it up this way:

- **Module 1**: Teach the concepts or big ideas a learner must understand to be able to perform the skill. If the concepts are complex, you will have to define them.[3]

- **Module 2**: Teach the basic things a learner must know/do/have to be able to perform the skill.

- **Module 3**: Take the learner through the steps of performing the skill.
- **Module 4**: Point out any modifications, clarifications, or exceptions to the rules you just taught.

For a Motor Skills (Movement) Course

If your course teaches physical movement, set it up like this:[4]

- **Module 1**: Teach each individual movement that is part of the movement routine.
- **Module 2**: Help learners put the movements together to create a smooth flow.
- **Module 3**: Help learners practice the movement routine.
- **Module 4**: Help learners get immediate feedback on how well they performed the routine. (You can use an app that films the learner to provide immediate remote feedback.)
- **Module 5**: Help learners continue to practice the routine both physically and via mental rehearsal (visualizing themselves performing the routine correctly).

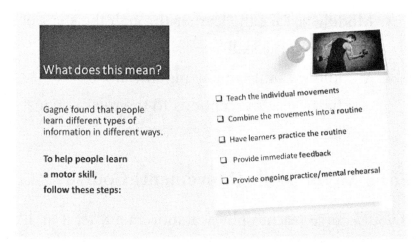

What does this mean?

Gagné found that people learn different types of information in different ways.

To help people learn a motor skill, follow these steps:

☐ Teach the individual movements

☐ Combine the movements into a routine

☐ Have learners practice the routine

☐ Provide immediate feedback

☐ Provide ongoing practice/mental rehearsal

Figure 7.7: How to set up a course that teaches motor skills (physical movement). (Source: Learn and Get Smarter, Inc./ Getty Images)

***

There is a free downloadable infographic on my website that you can use to remind you about how to set up the modules for a course in each of the five learning domains (see "Next Steps").

EIGHT

....

STEP 4: PLAN AND SET UP YOUR LESSONS

Take a deep breath and pat yourself on the back! You've accomplished a lot. First, you clarified the transformation you want your course to deliver. We talked about how to structure your course as a whole, to ensure it does indeed deliver the intended transformation.

Let's return to the metaphor of building a house, to help paint a mental picture of this step. (See figure 8.1 on the next page.)

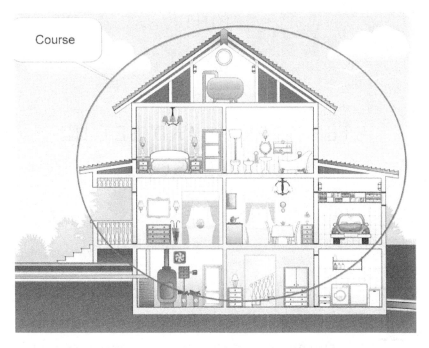

Course

Figure 8.1. Your course learning goal determines the overall shape of your course. (Source: Learn and Get Smarter, Inc./ Getty Images)

Next, you discovered the type of learning your course contains. Then, you set up your modules based on research into how people learn your exact type of course material best. (See figure 8.2 on the next page.)

At this stage, the heavy lifting is done. Your house is set up and framed!

Now we are going to lay out your lessons within each module. If you were building a house, this is the part where you would divide each floor of your house into separate rooms.

Modules

Figure 8.2. The modules in your course are like the floors in a house. (Source: Learn and Get Smarter, Inc./ Getty Images)

To set up your lessons within each module, treat each module as a separate minicourse and repeat the process you just went through when determining the nature of the overall course.

First, clarify the transformation the module delivers. (The module's transformation must lead directly to the overall transformation for the course as a whole.)

Then, determine the domain of learning for the module. For example, your course as a whole could be a how-to course, and within that how-to course your first

Figure 8.3. Your lessons are like the rooms on each floor of a house. (Source: Learn and Get Smarter, Inc./Getty Images)

module could consist of verbal information. So, you would set up that first module the correct way for teaching verbal information, by dividing the information up into smaller chunks (each chunk will become one lesson within the module).

Once you have the lessons laid out inside each module, the next step in the Course Design Formula® is to plan each lesson.

In order to do that, you need to understand how to set up a lesson plan.

Lesson Plans

Why do lessons have to be planned? Why can't they just happen spontaneously?

Let me ask you this. Would you like to live in a house that was built spontaneously, based on whatever the architect or builder felt like doing that day? Or would you rather live in a house that was built according to a plan?

Once the house is designed and built according to a solid plan, you can live inside it in a spontaneous way, but the actual design needs to be based on time-tested principles of what makes a house not fall down and go boom, right?

Having a house fall down while one is living in it is not the kind of spontaneity we want—and the same goes for having a lesson fall flat while your course participants are trying to learn from it. There will be plenty of room for spontaneity, discovery, and serendipity inside your lessons, once they've been carefully planned to promote effective learning.

So, how does one plan a lesson? As you'll recall, Gagné defined teaching as "arranging a series of events that promote learning."[1] He studied skilled teachers in action and observed that they all followed a series of procedures that he described as "the nine events of instruction."[2] The nine events are a series of steps that ensure the material you're teaching is effectively processed and learned.

We'll use the structure of these nine events to plan each and every lesson in your course. That way you can be sure that each lesson promotes learning in a way that moves your course participants closer to the transformation your course promises.

The Nine Events of Instruction

Presenting the instruction is the core activity in teaching anything to anyone, whether online or in person. When you present your instruction to your learners, you will present it differently if you are teaching an attitude, a cognitive strategy, a motor skill, and so on. But presenting the lesson material is actually only one of the nine phases of instruction.

The nine steps of instruction are steps skilled teachers have always taken. If you are a skilled teacher in classroom-based settings, you probably already follow these steps without having to stop and think about them.

The nine events of instruction remain the same no matter what type of learning you are presenting. But when you get to Step 4, "Present the Instruction," you will present the lesson material differently based on the domain of learning for the specific lesson you are teaching. The challenge in presenting instruction online is that, when the context changes, the things we have always done automatically may not work anymore.

When devising lesson plans, it is helpful to be able to consciously refer to a framework or checklist to be sure that we are not leaving anything out. We may need to adjust and adapt aspects of our instruction in order to make them work as well online as they did in the classroom.

Why Is It Important to Follow the Nine Events of Instruction?

Really learning something new is a bit like having a medical procedure. You enter into the learning experience in one condition and leave it in another (hopefully better) condition.

As with medical procedures, sometimes learning involves experiencing a bit of discomfort, because you can't learn anything new unless you are willing to step outside your comfort zone (just as you can't have a medical procedure unless you are willing to submit to it).

But as with medical procedures, real learning should not be painful. A skilled practitioner, whether educational or medical, needs to know how to help you move from your "before" state to your desired "after" state in a way that is relatively painless. In fact, the art of truly skilled teaching involves knowing how to help the learner get from their starting Point A to their desired Point B while experiencing a sense of enjoyment and excitement along the way.

When you go in for a medical procedure, the doctor does not meet you in the lobby armed with a sharp instrument and immediately begin poking around in your guts. That would not be surgery, it would be assault. There is a process you go through before, during, and after a medical procedure that ensures that everything goes smoothly, that the right procedure is done in the right way, and that you are on your road to healing with minimum pain and stress.

The same is true for educational procedures. There is a series of steps that need to be followed before, during, and after the actual instructional event that changes your brain. Even though these before and after steps are not the actual instruction, the instruction will not be effective unless all of these steps are followed—and in the right order.

Three Steps to Take Before You Present the Instruction (Events 1–3)

Steps taken before delivering the instruction are there to be sure that learners are fully present, are aware of what is going to be done, and have everything they need in order to get the most out of the learning experience.

Everything they need means: the prior knowledge necessary to allow the new information to be processed and stored in long-term memory.

If learners have the appropriate schemas based on prior learning in place, then learning something new will be relatively easy and fun for them. It will be like adding some new clothes to their existing closets or drawers (and who doesn't like getting new clothes to put in their closets, right?).

If it turns out that learners don't have any existing closets or drawers (schemas) to hold the new clothes (information), then they are going to have to build some. Building a closet from scratch takes a lot more work than just hanging up a new outfit in an existing closet. It takes a lot more work, but it can still be fun, as long as learners get the guidance and help they need from their instructor (that's you!) regarding how to do it.

If they don't have any preexisting closets or drawers (schemas) and they don't get help from their teacher in how to build any, they are just going to end up with a whole bunch of "clothes" (uncategorized information) dumped all over the place. The clothes (new information) won't get put away (stored in long-term memory) and there will be no good way to find or use those clothes (the information in the course) in the future.

They will have paid for the new clothes (paid for the online course) and then will not be able to actually find or wear them (they will not get anything out of the course).

We don't want that to happen to your students, which is why it's so important to get each of these steps of instruction right, starting from the very beginning.

Event 1: Gain the Learner's Attention

SEX!

(Made you look).

There you go. Oldest trick in the book, right?

OK, so now I have your attention . . . but in a minute you are going to be mad, because I used your biological instincts to get you to do something in a way that was manipulative and tricky.

Don't do that.

If your course is about the human reproductive system, then writing "*SEX*" in screaming letters across the top of the screen might be an appropriate way to get your learners' attention.

The real, professional, classy (and legal!) way to get your learners' attention is to understand that my (fake) headline screaming "*SEX!*" should be understood as a metaphor. You will get your learners' attention if you make it clear to them that your course is going to provide something that they want and need in order to make their lives better.

The reason your course is going to make your students' lives better is that they really are going to learn something in your course. Unlike my deliberately farfetched example, your course is going to actually deliver on the promises it makes.

So, how *do* you get your learners' attention? At the level of your course as a whole, one way to get their attention is through proper use of search engine optimization (SEO) and digital marketing techniques. You want your course to be visible to and gain the attention of the people you created it to help.

As you present the actual content within your course, think of gaining the learner's attention as the equivalent of presenting a tantalizing appetizer to whet a diner's interest in advance of the main dish of the meal. The goal is to get them focused, salivating, and hungry for the delectable intellectual entree that lies ahead.

Event 2: Tell Them What They Will Learn in This Lesson

At the level of each individual module or lesson within your course, you can gain learners' attention and inform them of the learning objective at the same time. Tell them what they are going to learn, how it will benefit them and help them get closer to their desired destination, Point B. What will they be able to do after completing this module, unit, or lesson that they can't do now? How fabulous and exciting will that be for them?

One way you can simultaneously gain learners' attention and tell them what they are going to learn is to present a short, self-scoring online quiz or challenge inviting them to perform the skill they will be learning about in this lesson.

Examples:

- "Can you stand on one foot for two minutes without losing your balance?"
- "How many of the capitals of Europe do you know?"
- "Do you wish you could balance your checkbook in your sleep?"

- "How fabulous would it be to lose weight and keep it off, without feeling hungry?"

That's the gaining attention part.

Then, once you've got the learners' attention, tell them how the specific content of this course, module, or lesson will make it possible for them to do that very thing that they are not able to do now. For example:

- "In this course, we will learn five techniques for improving balance on each side of the body."
- "By the time you are done with this lesson, you will know the capital of every country in the world."
- "What I am about to teach you will put your financial record keeping on autopilot for the rest of your life."
- "Dr. Smith's program has helped thousands of people lose weight and keep it off. We will explore all phases of his program in this course. Let's start right now by learning which foods are allowed, which aren't, and why."

Don't just say it will be fabulous and exciting. Spell out specifically how the learning in this module or lesson is going to help them get closer to their goal and fulfill the promise you made to them—and the promise they made to themselves—when they signed up for your course.

As you begin each specific learning experience within each lesson (meaning, as you begin each video, PowerPoint, PDF, or other piece of instructional content), it is a good practice to briefly explain to the learner exactly what the purpose of this specific piece of content is and how it relates to the overall course goal.

It's especially important to do this if the relationship between a specific lesson and the larger course goal is not immediately obvious. For example, let's say your course is about meditation, and within that course you are presenting a video that demonstrates proper breathing technique. You might open the video by saying something like this: "In this lesson, we are going to focus on proper breathing technique. Breathing technique is very important for learning meditation because it helps you relax."

Or: "Breathing techniques have traditionally been the first thing taught in many meditation disciplines because it is thought that life energy enters and leaves the body's subtle energy centers along with the breath."

As you can see, there is a relationship between gaining the learner's attention and making them aware of the learning objective.

If the learner does not see how a specific lesson relates to the overall learning goal, they may decide to skip it, using a rationale such as, "I want to learn meditation, not breathing! I already know how to breathe. I'll just skip ahead to the next video."

One way to counteract the tendency to skip ahead is to begin the next video with a reminder that knowing proper breathing technique is required prior knowledge for the new thing you are going to teach. That way, even if a learner does skip ahead to the next video, you will be able to catch them and direct them back to the earlier lesson on breathing techniques, so they don't miss out on the prior knowledge they need for the step that follows.

Event 3: Help Learners Focus on Their Prior Relevant Knowledge

Someone once said that if a job is really hard, somewhere there is a tool that will make it really easy. Having the right prior knowledge is the single most important determinant of how easily and well someone will be able to learn something new.

When the hard job is learning something new, the tool that makes it really easy is having the right prior knowledge.

A lot of the art of teaching so that people really learn resides in correctly identifying the prior knowledge your learners need, and then ensuring that they have it. If your learners don't already have the prior knowledge they need to learn the new subject matter, then the art of teaching consists in building that necessary prior knowledge directly into the structure of your lesson.

How do you identify the prior knowledge your learners must have to ensure they are ready to understand, absorb and benefit from what you are about to teach them? In a face-to-face classroom, where you would be in constant interaction with your learners in real time, you could determine the answer to that question directly, by asking your students questions, by noticing where they get lost or stuck, and so on.

But in an online course, you are creating a single set of lessons that need to work consistently for all of your learners all the time, forever. Because it takes a lot of effort and resources to design online-learning materials, it is discouraging to need to redo them later. For this reason, course designers are often reluctant to change their course materials once these have been "engraved in concrete."

In addition, while ongoing revision in response to learner feedback is an important part of an online course's evolution and growth, even the initial presentation of an online course needs to be much more of a "finished product" than a live classroom presentation ever is. You do not want your learners to draw a blank stare on day one of your course because they lack the prior knowledge needed to benefit from what you are trying to teach them.

The way to avoid the need for revisions is to follow the principle used by tailors and carpenters for millennia, "Measure twice, cut once." Measure by applying some careful preplanning to the design of your course as a whole and of each lesson and each piece of content within the course in particular.

The way to do that is to start with the course goal (what will your learners be able to do after taking your course, that they could not do before?) and work backward step by step to be sure you are very clear on all the prior knowledge needed for each lesson.

Then, when you actually teach the course, you can just move forward through that same sequence of steps. You will have the necessary prior knowledge needed for each lesson spelled out clearly, and you can share what the prior knowledge is with your learners as you teach.

Let's look at a specific example to understand how this is going to work. I'm randomly picking a course topic out of the air: "How to Bake a Cake."

Question 1: What is the course goal? (Meaning: What will learners be able to do after completing the course that they can't do now?)

Answer: The learners will be able to bake a cake.

That seems simple enough, but there are some other things we need to know before we can delve deeper, such as:

- How well will the learner be able to bake a cake?
- Under what conditions?
- Using what equipment?

How's this: Given a cake recipe, raw ingredients, an oven, and baking utensils, learners will be able to bake a cake that at least 80 percent of their friends and family eat without coercion and pronounce "delicious."

The sentence above is called a *student learning objective* or *instructional objective.*

You can create your own student learning objectives using this handy Mad Lib®-style student-learning-objective generator that I've created just for you.

"Given _____, *students will be able to* _____ *to* _____ *standards of achievement, as demonstrated by* _____*."*

Now, if your final course goal is for students to be able to bake an edible cake, what are the smaller lesson goals leading up to that? You can see from your learning objective that students will need to be able to:

- Read a recipe.
- Identify and obtain raw ingredients.
- Operate an oven.
- Identify and use baking utensils.

That is the prior knowledge your learners will need to have in order to accomplish the course goal. From this list, you can see that a logical lesson sequence for your course would be:

1. Read the recipe.
2. Get the ingredients.
3. Prepare the ingredients.
4. Bake the cake.
5. Cool the cake.
6. Frost and decorate the cake.

7. Invite people to eat the cake. (I'm getting hungry just thinking about this, are you?)

Let's look at the first lesson you need to design, "How to Read a Recipe."

What prior knowledge must your students have in order to learn how to read a recipe? Any ideas? Well, yes, they must already know how to read! It will not be possible for your students to read a recipe if they are unable to read at all.

So, how would you remind your learners of the relevant prior knowledge they need?

You might mention that they have done various kinds of reading in their lives, and now they are going to focus on a specific kind of reading that will help them make a cake. You might mention some of the factors that make recipe reading different from other kinds of reading, such as the fact that recipes are sets of directions for how to cook something, and that recipes tend to be very precise. You also might mention that recipes are often found together in collections called "cookbooks." In addition, you might mention that sometimes people don't have all the items available that a recipe calls for, and therefore cookbooks sometimes will offer readers lists of acceptable substitutions somewhere in the book—often at the back.

This is just an example, and a deliberately simplistic one at that. Your content will vary depending on the specific subject matter of your course.

My point here is to show you how to move backward from your overall course goal to your course learning objective, and then to your lesson sequence in order to discover the exact prior knowledge your learners will need in order to benefit from each lesson.

As you plan your course in detail, you will write all of this down. You'll be creating a set of notes for yourself that will help you focus your learners' attention on the relevant prior knowledge they need for each lesson in your course. The best time to help learners access their relevant prior knowledge is just before you begin teaching the new lesson material.

What you are doing is helping people bring the schemas they have already built, which are relevant to what you are about to teach, to the forefront of their minds. That way they will have mental storage bins ready and waiting to catch the new information you're presenting.

An added benefit of reminding your learners of the prior knowledge they need is that it provides a natural segue leading directly into the lesson material itself.

What If the Prior Knowledge Is Too Easy or Too Hard?

In the example I just gave about how to bake a cake, we focused on knowing how to read a recipe as important prior knowledge. As you were reading, you might have been thinking, *"This is ridiculous! All my students already know how to read recipes. I don't need to teach them that!"*

Or if your target audience is made up of nonreaders for any reason, you might have been thinking, *"That's too hard! My students can't read. They are going to learn how to bake a cake by watching me do it using videos. Reading recipes is not part of what I need them to be focusing on."*

Either of those responses could be valid depending on what you are teaching and to whom. The prior knowledge needed for your lessons will vary depending on both the subject matter and the nature of your audience. Only you, as the course creator, can determine what is appropriate and needed for your specific course.

Another point is that *some* of your students might already know how to read a recipe while others might need to learn.

You could also find that you have a sub-group of students who will never be able to read a printed recipe. Perhaps they are blind, do not speak English, or have severe dyslexia. Yet they still want to be able to learn how to bake a cake by taking your online course.

This is where it comes in handy to provide your lessons in multiple formats.

Being able to read a recipe is helpful for baking a cake, but it's not essential. If reading a recipe is out of the question, a learner could listen to an audio version of the recipe instead, for example.

One way to handle the variability of your learners' needs in an online setting would be to create a separate minicourse (or even a separate full-length course) on how to read a recipe, including information on how to access recipes in alternate ways (such as audio) if reading a recipe is not an option for any reason. You could then offer this separate course on recipe reading as an option for those of your students who need it.

Another option is to create a list of links and resources on recipe reading that your students can explore on their own to refresh their understanding, before diving into your course material.

***

We've now discussed the three steps that Gagné found highly effective teachers take before they begin delivering new lesson material. Effective teachers make sure they have the students' attention, make sure their students are clear on what they are about to learn, and make sure students can access relevant prior knowledge needed for the upcoming lesson. Once all that has been taken care of, it's time to move directly into actually teaching the lesson. Both your students and you will be primed and ready to do so!

Three Steps to Take *While* You Present the Instruction (Events 4–6)

We've reached a point that is exciting for any course creator—actually presenting instruction to learners! Notice how long it took us to get to this point. There is a reason for that, which is, that if you want your learners to really benefit from the instruction, you need to take specific steps both before and after actually presenting the instruction, in order for your learners to benefit from it.

Remember the analogy I mentioned earlier, that learning is somewhat like having a medical procedure? When you go in for a medical procedure, the actual medical part in which you are dressed in a paper sheet being poked at with sharp implements is not the first thing that happens (that would be assault), nor is it the last thing that happens (that would be indecent exposure, combined with some degree of hemorrhage).

While this example might be a bit exaggerated (or a bit understated, depending on whether the medical procedure is a mole extraction or open-heart surgery), it is here to remind you that immediately presenting instruction without the proper preparation and follow through is not the most effective way to teach. If you want to make sure that your learners really benefit from your instruction, it's important to follow these steps in the right order. It may take a bit longer to prepare your instruction when you do it this way, but it is well worth it.

Let's revisit our house metaphor for a moment. Let's say your dream for your house is to sit at your desk looking out the window while you write. That's a wonderful dream, but would you rush out to buy glass for the window (that doesn't exist yet) and buy a desk (for the study that has no walls yet) as the first step? No. You would first have to build the house, put in the floors, frame the windows, add flooring, insulate the walls, and so on. You would be patient about taking all those preparatory steps, because you would understand why they are necessary.

The same is true as you lay the foundations for your online course. First you have to frame it correctly and set it up right. Then you have to plan your lessons. Then you have to select your media—which is what we're about to do—before you will be ready at last to actually create your lessons.

Event 4: Present the Instruction

The steps we've discussed so far apply to any type of learning in any learning domain. It does not matter if you are teaching verbal information, an attitude, a cognitive strategy, an intellectual skill, or a motor skill. Before you present the instruction, you will need to take the same three preliminary steps.

Now we are up to the part where you actually teach a specific lesson. Because we are talking about teaching in the context of designing an online course, teaching a specific lesson means planning and designing the multimedia lesson materials that will carry the instructional content of the course from your mind to your learner's mind. If you do this right, the end result will be a wonderful aha moment when your learner suddenly "gets it."

To ensure maximum learning, the way you will present the instruction must vary, depending on the domain of learning that your course, lesson, or specific piece of multimedia content falls into. The first thing you must do is determine the domain of learning of each part of your instructional sequence.

Trust me. The effort is worth it. Here's why you can and should do as I suggest. Everything I am about to share with you I learned the hard way—and sometimes the *very hard way*—from designing my master's project in instructional technology. I used a process known as *rapid prototyping* to design different versions of my lesson materials.[3] I kept going until I reached a "failure point" beyond which it was not possible to continue because the lesson had stopped working. The process was messy, slow, frustrating, and inefficient. Every time I reached a failure point, I had to go back and start over until I was able to design a lesson all the way through in a way that worked.[4]

Thomas Edison is famous for having tried 10,000 things that did not work before he came up with the one thing that did work to invent the light bulb. The end result of all those failures and all his frustrating trial and error was that he ended up with something amazing that has been lighting up our lives for the past 150 years. While you are not inventing the light

Figure 8.4. The goal of your online course is to create light-bulb moments. (Source: Getty Images)

bulb, you are creating a way for metaphorical light bulbs to go off over your students' heads.

For all true educators, this is why we teach. This is what we live for.

The failure points I reached trying to use various methods in my project showed me that the steps that follow are the most efficient way to get a light-bulb moment to happen for any kind of subject matter and using any kind of lesson material in an online teaching context.

Event 5: Provide Guided Practice

Presenting the instruction is the heart of the teaching experience, but it is only one of the nine steps that Gagné observed good teachers following in order to make the instruction stick. If you just present the instruction and walk away, your instruction may fly right out of your students' heads after you're done. If you want the instruction to stick, you have to do specific things after your lesson presentation to cement the learning.

Right after you present the instruction by teaching the new content that is the heart of the lesson, it is important to help students practice using the content with your guidance.

Guided practice will look different depending on the domain of learning. For example, if you are teaching verbal information, guided practice could look like:

- **Presenting the lesson:** You explain that the days of the week are called Monday, Tuesday, Wednesday, Thursday, Friday, Saturday, and Sunday.

- **Guided practice:** You ask the students to repeat the days of the week after you, one at a time.

That type of rote repetition can certainly be effective. But is it exciting, engaging, and interesting? (Yawn.) Guided practice is where you have the opportunity to make your instruction really pop. How? You can increase student engagement with the learning task (germane cognitive load) by moving up the levels of Bloom's taxonomy.

Let's take a minute to refresh our memory of Bloom's taxonomy. (See what I did there? I'm reminding you of your relevant prior knowledge.) In Part One, we discussed how Bloom's taxonomy classifies and organizes learners' ways of processing information from the most basic to the most advanced. The taxonomy organizes thinking skills into two major groups: lower- and higher-order thinking skills.[5]

Lower-order thinking skills include remembering, understanding, and applying what was learned. Many lessons, both online and offline, don't go beyond that point. But to truly engage learners and make sure the subject matter has been permanently stored in their long-term memory, it's important also to include higher-order thinking skills, such as analyzing the new information, evaluating it (or using it to evaluate other things), and finally, creating something new that shows the learners they've truly achieved their learning goal.

The great news for online course creators is that the online-learning environment makes it very easy for learners to engage in higher-order thinking skills and discover for themselves how much they have gained from a lesson. But there is one big, gigantic *if*. The online learning environment makes it very easy for learners to engage in higher-order thinking skills, *if* the course creator builds activities into the lessons to encourage that.

And here we are: You, the course creator, are at the point of building activities into your lesson to help your students go over the new material you've just taught them. Even with something as simple as learning the names of the days of the week (which you probably would not be teaching to adult learners in their native language, but might be teaching in a foreign language class), you can make the guided practice part of your lesson engaging and fun by creating activities that require your students to use higher-order thinking skills.

For example, instead of just having students parrot back the names of the days of the week, you could have them either write in (or drag and drop) the names onto the correct spots of a fillable PDF calendar.

(As you skillfully plan your lesson sequence, each of these steps will lead to the next. Upcoming steps in this lesson will have learners print out the calendar and use it for a week to actually write down their daily activities. At the end of the week, they will write a brief summary of everything they did on each day that week, using the correct names of the days in the target language. Do you see how much more engaging and involving that would be than simply having them repeat the day names back to you? Students are more likely to remember the names of the days of the week once they have a personal, tangible experience of associating those names with the actual activities they did on those days in real life.)

Providing guided practice to your students is important for solid learning. You want to be sure that as they start using the new material you've just taught them, they do it right. It's important not to allow them to reinforce mistakes accidentally.

Now let's move on to the next step in the lesson sequence: independent performance.

Event 6: Help Learners Perform on Their Own

Now that your students have had a chance to practice using the new information in your lesson with direct guidance from you, it's time for them to do it on their own.

We're using an imaginary example lesson in which you taught them the days of the week in a foreign language. You provided them with guided practice by allowing them to copy a sample weekly calendar you provided, filling in their own PDF calendars with the correct names for the days of the week in the target language.

Now you are going to have them independently use the calendar they created by asking them to actually write down daily tasks they do each day that week in real time.

The point here is to carefully structure an activity that forces your learners to use the new information you presented in your most recent lesson, on their own, without guidance from you. In this case, for one whole day this coming week, your learners will be staring at the day name in the target language every time they look at their calendar. But you won't be staring over their shoulders. Instead, your learners will be using the new information you've just taught them, on their own, independently, out in the real world.

This is the point you want your learners to get to, by the end of the "during the instruction" phase of the Nine Steps of Instruction.

Let's review the steps of lesson creation so far, using an example lesson from a different domain of learning. We explored teaching the days of the week in a foreign language, which is verbal information. Now let's see how you might teach a cognitive strategy. Cognitive strategies are ways of learning how to learn. Let's say that this next imaginary course you are creating is "How to Ace the LSAT" (the standardized law school admissions test).

Let's say your goal for your first lesson is to have each student select an LSAT prep book to purchase and use to prepare for the exam. You've presented the instruction by showing your online students all the current books on the market for LSAT preparation. Having presented the instruction (the information about the prep books), you could set up the guided practice part of the lesson by having students read online reviews of those books and then fill in a checklist you've created for them, which will enable them to compare the features of each book. The checklist enforces guided practice by requiring students to look for the specific features of each LSAT book that you consider important for mastering the exam. The checklist you provide will help your students notice whether each book does or does not provide the important exam prep features.

Reviewing Bloom's taxonomy again, we remind ourselves of the following.

Lower-order thinking skills include:

- Remembering.
- Understanding.
- Applying what was learned.

Higher-order thinking skills include:

- Analyzing new information.
- Evaluating it (or using it to evaluate other things).
- Creating something new that demonstrates the learning that has taken place.

In the guided practice part of your lesson, where you will have your students fill in a checklist about the features of each book based on the reviews they've read, you are asking them to remember, understand, and apply what they've learned from reading book reviews. In other words, they will be using lower-order thinking skills.

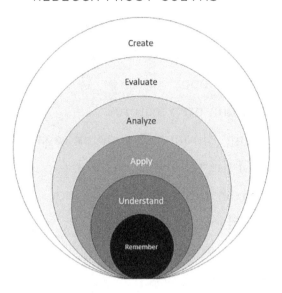

Figure 8.5. Bloom's revised taxonomy. (Source: Learn and Get Smarter, Inc.)

When you are ready to help them move into the independent performance part of the lesson, you could have them participate in a group discussion (using an online forum) or create a class *wiki* (a shared, editable document) in which they compare and contrast the features of each LSAT exam prep book with other students, come to a conclusion about which book will work best for them to master the LSAT, and defend their decision to the group. These activities will require the use of higher-order thinking skills.

The activities are engaging (they have optimal germane cognitive load) because each student will decide which LSAT prep book will work best for them, personally, to achieve an important life goal. The discussion format is participatory and interactive and makes good use of the affordances of the online learning space.

These are just examples of what you could do in your lesson plan, of course. You will design your course, your way, for your students and your subject matter. What I want you to notice is how much power and control you have to design your lessons in engaging, interactive, and transformative ways, once you understand and take control of the following things:

- **What is the domain of learning?** You will design your guided practice and independent performance portions of each lesson based on the specific type of learning involved.

- **What step of the lesson are you designing?** There's a difference between presenting new information, providing guided practice, and helping students perform independently. Be very clear on exactly which step of the lesson you are on, and then design your instruction specifically to accomplish the mission of that step.

- **How can you reduce and balance cognitive load?** Focus tightly on the exact information you are teaching in the specific lesson. Put that information in an easy-to-open package (lesson format). Make opening the lesson package exciting, interactive, and fun for your learners, using the specific things that online learning makes it easy to do.

- **Are you helping learners use higher-order thinking skills?** This is where online learning really shines, because the online learning space makes it easy for students to analyze, evaluate, and create new things—but only if you, the course creator, set your lessons up that way.

Steps to Take *After* You Present the Instruction (Events 7–9)

You've taught your lesson. You've presented the new material, helped your students practice what you've preached, and structured in ways for them to continue to practice using the lesson material on their own.

And yet, even after all that, your work is not done.

There are a few important considerations to keep in mind at this point in the teaching and learning sequence. Your learners have been using, repeating, practicing, and working with the new information you've given them. They have practiced with your direct help and on their own. But since they are just learning this as new material, they need to be clear on whether they are doing all this correctly.

They need feedback and guidance on how they are doing and on whether corrections need to be made in their performance of the learning task.

They also need some kind of objective assessment to let them know where they stand.

And finally, they need help in taking what you've taught them out into the real world and using it—applying it in various situations or under various conditions.

The three steps of instruction that you take after the main instructional part of the lesson are designed to accomplish these tasks.

Event 7: Provide Learners with Feedback on How Well They Did

As you design each lesson in your online course, you need to structure in ways for students to get feedback on whether they have correctly performed the learning task that was taught in that lesson.

Check every lesson to make sure it includes some way for learners to know whether they've achieved the learning objective for that lesson. (In order for them to achieve it, the lesson must have a clear learning objective to begin with!)

If they have performed a new skill correctly, learners need to know why their performance was good. What specific things did they do right? That way, they can focus on doing those specific things in the right way again in the future until their performance truly becomes automatic.

If there are aspects of their performance that need to improve, what are those aspects? And in what specific ways do they need to improve?

To see how this works, let's use an example imaginary course that teaches motor skills: "How to Rock the Tango."

You've gotten your students' attention by showing them a dramatic video of the grand masters of tango doing an enchanting dance.

You've informed them of the learning objective for this lesson, which is to learn how to do a dramatic dip where the gentleman bends way over the lady as she bends over backward . . . yet neither of them (hopefully!) falls to the ground.

You've also refreshed their memory of their prior knowledge of other dance steps and postures that they will need to keep in mind as they learn this new step.

Then you've taught them the new step (presented the instruction).

For guided practice, maybe you used a video, maybe you included PDFs, or possibly you had them download paper templates of feet to place at specific locations on their floor at home to actually practice the steps.

For independent performance, maybe you assigned them the task of locating several YouTube videos that show the move in question and asked them to find a partner and practice what they see in those videos (in several different styles) until they can do the move smoothly on their own.

So far so good. Your students are up and running (off and dancing) with at least a rudimentary ability to perform the step in question. Or so one hopes. But how can you be sure your students are doing it right? More important, how can *they* be sure?

This is where the next step, providing feedback, comes in. The purpose of feedback is to let learners know whether they are on track to achieve the learning goal. If the feedback tells them they are on track, they can keep going. If the feedback tells them they are off track, they can circle back to review earlier parts of the lesson before they get too far afield.

Feedback is related to assessment, but the two are not exactly the same. Here's a simple way to think of the difference: Feedback lets you know how you're doing, while assessment tells you how you did. Feedback lets you know whether you're on track and on target to achieve a learning goal. Assessment tells you whether you've successfully achieved it.

You can use a type of assessment as a way to provide feedback while a course is in process. That type of in-progress assessment is called *formative assessment,* while the final assessment at the end of a course is called *summative assessment.*

There are several different kinds of feedback your students can receive in an online course.

- They can do an in-progress self-assessment, such as videotaping their movements and then comparing their version to the YouTube video models.
- They can do a peer assessment. For example, you could have students email or text links to their videos to each other, or post them on a class forum, to receive critiques and suggestions for improvement from other students.
- Or you as the instructor can be the one to provide the feedback. In order to do that, you

have to structure in some way for you to be able to see what your students' performance looks like. You could ask them to email you a link to their videos of themselves dancing. You could have them post links to the videos to a forum or wiki. You could set up a time to watch each student perform the dance steps live via Skype, Zoom, Facetime, or any other video-conferencing site.

An advantage of the live video conference option would be that your feedback can be immediate, taking place while your students are actually performing the dance. It is a general principle of good instruction that the more immediate the feedback, the more helpful it is.

Have you ever had the experience of turning in an assignment and then waiting for weeks to get it back? Even if it comes back loaded with helpful comments from your instructor, those comments are so far removed from the time you completed the assignment that they are of less value than immediate feedback would have been.

Immediate feedback is especially important when teaching movement activities, such as how to rock the tango. You want to immediately and specifically correct any improper movements and make sure your students are getting the steps down right, so they can train their muscle memory to be able to perform the movements correctly.

As you design each lesson, think about not only what you will teach but how you will observe your students' performance (or help them observe it for themselves) so they can get immediate feedback on how they are doing.

In doing so, keep in mind the affordances and constraints of online learning, as well as your own capabilities as an instructor. For example, online learning affords you the ability to reach thousands of students worldwide with a single course.

Now, what does that mean for providing feedback? Well, as we just saw, providing immediate feedback via videoconferencing would be an excellent way to provide feedback to your students in a dance course. But realistically, if you did have *thousands* of students, you, as a *single* instructor, would not have enough time to set up a video conference with each one.

What you could do instead would be to provide a checklist of specific things to look for in their performance and then have students conduct a self-assessment first by comparing their own videotaped performance to one you create for them, followed by a peer assessment in the form of a live video conference with another student. You could then set up an asynchronous question and answer forum so that students who have specific questions or things they would like you to look at, could ask for additional help.

If you start to see that a lot of students have the same kinds of questions, you could create mini-lessons to address each one of those issues specifically, and include them in your FAQs or a special section on "Things to watch for" or "Tango dip tips and tricks."

If the nature of your subject matter allows it, you can provide your learners with immediate feedback after every lesson or even after each piece of content within each lesson, by creating a short (one- or two-question) self-scoring, no-credit quiz. This will provide immediate feedback without you, the instructor, having to be directly involved. This is one of the truly fantastic affordances of the online-learning medium, so use it to your, and your students', advantage.

One of the issues I am hearing from students who have taken online courses is that they felt they did not receive enough support and feedback from their instructors. Providing feedback is important not only for student success, but also for student satisfaction with your course. Your students are working hard to change their brains and learn something new. While doing so, they are placing themselves in a vulnerable position. Feeling that their instructor sees their efforts and provides specific and supportive guidance on how they are doing is a critical aspect of the learning process. In terms of sales of a course, you also do not want your students to be so dissatisfied they want their money back. In terms of marketing, you want them to give your course positive—even rave—reviews. Building ongoing feedback into your learning design so that your students feel seen and supported at every step of their learning journey is an important way to ensure your learners experience you and your course in the most positive possible light.

A key to providing effective and satisfying feedback is to make it encouraging, performance-based, specific, timely, and clear. For a preschooler doing a painting, saying, "The way you made the sun bright orange makes me feel so warm and happy" provides more useful feedback than saying "That's pretty!" or "I like that!" or "You're such a good painter!"

For students in middle school or high school you could say, "I can see that you really worked hard learning these verb conjugations. You did a great job conjugating the regular verb [insert regular verb here] and you got it completely right. Now here's a challenge for you . . . can you conjugate the verb [*insert irregular verb here*]? That one is irregular so it's trickier, but I think you can handle it. Are you up for the challenge?"

For college students and adults, find out what their goals are for why they are pursuing the course of study. That helps align feedback to the reason they are taking the course, making it more meaningful to them. It's not one person "judging" another, but rather someone they have selected to help them achieve their goals, providing helpful information as to how they are doing on achieving those goals.

Event 8: Help Learners Assess Their Learning and Performance

Ah, assessment. This is where the rubber meets the road in online (and all other) forms of learning. The moment of truth is at hand. Did your students benefit from all the hard work you put into creating your online class? Have they actually learned what you've been trying to teach them?

You've created your lesson plan, clarified your learning objective, and built in activities to help your students perform the activities you are teaching them. Now you need to be sure there is some way to prove (to your students and yourself) that they've actually learned what you've been trying to teach them.

Rubrics. In creating assessments for your course, it's important to be clear on the exact learning you are evaluating. The best way to clarify this, for yourself and your learners, is to create a rubric. A rubric is a chart that lists the skills you expect your learners to develop, the behaviors you expect them to exhibit, or the activities you expect them to perform.

To set up a rubric, create a document with rows and columns giving you a series of boxes. A table that you can create in a text document works very well for this. I've created a blank template you can fill in to create your own rubric. You can download this on my website (see "Next Steps").

Use the boxes in the first column (down the left side of the table) to write the individual skills, behaviors, or activities your learners must complete in order to achieve the learning goal for your lesson. (You can also create rubrics for each module, and for your course as a whole, if you want). Use the boxes in the first row along the top of your table, to write your evaluation scale (for example: Poor/Fair/Good/ Excellent, or 1 point/2 points/3 points/4 points/5 points). Then fill in the boxes to the right of each skill, in a way that makes it clear what constitutes poor, fair, good, or excellent performance of that skill.

The following table (see pages 212–214) illustrates the general way rubrics work. The following example rubric is for a course on how to bake a cake. Yours can have fewer or more columns or rows, and the subject matter will vary depending on your course.

For the purpose of teaching ungraded courses that people are taking online (to improve their health, relationships, productivity, professional skills, and more), it might be more helpful to the learner to use a suggested follow-up activity, rather than a numerical point score, to let them know where they stand for each level of performance. For example, if the learner is completely unable to perform the skill, your suggestion could be for them to go back and take an earlier, more basic course.

If they are able to perform the skill, but not perfectly, your suggestion could be for them to review the previous materials in this current course.

If the learner is able to perform the skill perfectly, your suggestion could be that they are now ready to move on to the next lesson and/or take your next course.

Performance Standards	Just starting out	Getting there	Got it
SKILLS: 1. Assemble the ingredients.	You have downloaded the list of ingredients from the course. You have checked off those items you already have.	You have planned how to get the items you still need. You have shared your plan in the class discussion group.	You have all the ingredients. You have posted a picture of your ingredients to the class discussion group. You have provided feedback to two other students.

Performance Standards:	Just starting out	Getting there	Got it
2. Prepare to bake the cake	You have watched the "Baking Basics" video.	You have taken the "Baking Basics" quiz and gotten 100 percent. (You can retake the quiz as many times as needed to improve your score.)	You have applied the Baking Basics by: • Separating wet and dry ingredients. • Preheating the oven. • Greasing the pan.

Performance Standards:	Just starting out	Getting there	Got it
3. Bake and serve the cake	You have followed the steps of the recipe in Module 3 of this course.	You have filmed yourself baking the cake and talking through each step to explain what you're doing. (Put camera on tripod).	You have served your cake to three friends and filmed their reactions. You have posted both of your films to the class forum.

As you can see, a rubric not only helps your learners assess how they are doing in regard to performing each skill in your class, but also helps you determine which other courses, if any, you want to create as either precursors or follow-ups to the current one.

The important point is for your students to experience that you care about the quality of their learning experience at every step of the course. They need to know that it matters to you that they are learning, and that you are there to help them handle and overcome any challenges they may run into so that they can succeed in learning what they came to your course to learn.

Types of Assessment

There are different types of assessment you can build into your course, to help students know if they are achieving the learning goal. These include self-assessment, peer-assessment, instructor assessment, and automated assessment. Let's explore how each of these types of assessment could work.

Self-Assessment. A self-assessment can help your students determine whether, and to what degree, they have achieved the learning objective for the lesson. Activities such as keeping a reflective journal or making a list of things that work and things that don't work for each lesson facilitate self-assessment by helping learners reflect on their learning experience for each lesson and activity.

The learning objective for our imaginary cake-baking course states that learners will learn how to bake a cake that their friends and family will love. Let's say that you are planning the final lesson in this imaginary course. The final lesson, "Serving the Cake," requires the learners to serve the cake to at least three people who spontaneously declare it delicious in some way, as documented by candid video evidence.

The activity of serving the cake and observing people's reactions to it is the assessment not only for this final lesson but also for the course as a whole. It is a self-assessment in the sense that learners will be able to observe for themselves if they have accomplished what they set out to do when they signed up for the course. They will also be assessing whether they have completed all the activities involved in sharing their cake and recording their family's reaction, as specified in this final lesson plan.

Peer Assessment. The cake tasting is also a peer assessment, because the learners' family members and friends will be letting them know if the cakes they make pass muster or not. Usually, in an online class, peer assessment would involve the learners' classmates, rather than family and friends. But since pleasing family and friends was a built-in feature of the learning objective for this course, this is a valid peer assessment in this case.

If your online course has multiple students who all sign up and proceed through the lesson sequence at the same rate of speed, you can structure peer assessments into individual lessons, as well as into the course as a whole. The advantage of peer assessments is that they increase interaction among students. You can use features such as wikis, forums, private groups you create for your class on Facebook or another social network, and many other methods to promote peer assessment.

An advantage of peer assessments is that they relieve the instructor of the need to evaluate a huge number of students, if the course is very large—while still providing each student with some degree of objective external evaluation of their performance.

Be mindful, however, that students often do not find peer assessment an adequate substitute for the type of response they are hoping to get from their instructors.[6]

The type of online courses that I am assuming most readers of this book plan to create do not require formal letter grades. But in a course that does, it would be unfair to a student to have their grade depend on the evaluation skills and biases of a small subset of their fellow students, rather than having a standard-grading system provided by the instructor.

Even in an informal assessment situation, some students will be skilled at giving objective, criterion-based assessment using insightful and empathetic feedback, while others will not. If you are going to use peer assessment, it's important to provide guidelines as well as scoring or grading criteria in the form of a checklist or rubric that you provide to all students.

The subject matter of some online courses may make peer assessment inadvisable due to privacy issues. For example, if the topic of your course relates to something personal, it may be better to use self-assessment via a reflective journal—to allow each student to process the material in a private way.

Another problem with using peer assessment in an online class is that students may have signed up at different times or they may be moving through the lessons at different rates of speed. They may not all live in the same time zone, speak the same language, or share the same cultural assumptions about how assessment and evaluation should work. People in some cultures care only about results, whereas people in others focus more on the process used to arrive at the results. In some cultures, a less-than-perfect score or performance could be experienced as shameful, whereas in others it is considered helpful to point out all possible flaws in an attempt to make the final result even better.

My suggestion is to use peer assessment judiciously. If you are teaching the kind of class where fostering social interaction and/or group work on projects are important goals, then peer assessment can help promote those goals. On the other hand, if the nature of your course requires student performance to be evaluated objectively against a uniform benchmark, then instructor assessment or automated assessment are likely to be more effective and more appreciated by your students.

Instructor Assessment. Instructor assessment is self-explanatory: The instructor provides some kind of formal evaluation of the student's performance.

These final (summative) assessments serve a dual function. They provide individual students with formal evaluations of their own performances, and they provide the instructor with feedback about the degree to which the class as a whole has been able to achieve the learning objective for the course.

Automated Assessment. Educational testing is a highly developed field. When students are taking tests such as the SAT, GRE, LSAT, certifying exams for professional licensing and advancement, and so on, the stakes are very high. The tests used to provide these types of certifications are carefully, scientifically designed according to formal research methodology. If the online course you are developing requires that level of formal, rigorous assessment, the information you will need to design those types of assessments goes beyond the scope of this book.

But most online courses designed outside of a university or corporate setting won't require the level of test development that goes into designing an LSAT or SAT exam. (If your online course teaches a cognitive strategy such as how to prepare for those types of exams, there are preexisting practice samples of those specific tests that you could have your students use for their final assessment.)

So, what types of automated assessments can you use for your online course? Many internet-based course platforms come with self-scoring quiz or test features built in. You just have to determine the question type for your quiz or test (such as essay, multiple choice, and so on) and then populate the quiz with your own questions.

There can be a blurred line between automatic assessment (conducted entirely by the software once you set it up) and instructor assessment, which requires you as the instructor to review and evaluate your students' performance. Some quiz and test features available in online course platforms give you the option to include both types of questions in the same exam. For example, in Moodle you can have some multiple choice questions that are scored automatically by the software, along with some essay questions that can only be scored by the instructor.[7]

If you anticipate having a very large number of students in your course, you will save yourself time and stress by making the assessment entirely self-scoring and automatic. On the other hand, if the nature of your course requires close review or interaction between you and your students, you might find instructor assessment (or instructor review of partially automated assessment) works better for you and your students.

Assessment Across the Domains of Learning

If your course (or any component within the course) teaches **verbal information,** you can assess whether learners have achieved the learning goal by having them use words in some form to tell you what they've learned. The assessment can be simple (being able to recite a few words from memory) or complex (being able to write an essay comparing the ideas of multiple schools of thought).

To assess a **cognitive strategy,** have learners actually use the strategy and then see if it worked to help them learn what they are trying to learn.

To assess an **attitude** change, you will have to observe the learners' behavior over a long period of time. (They can't prove they've changed their attitude about smoking by simply saying so. Others have to be able to observe that they no longer smoke, for a long period of time.)

An authentic activity, either in the real world (baking a cake) or online (creating a course) makes a wonderful final assessment for an **intellectual skills** course. If you are teaching someone how to do something, the ultimate assessment is whether they are actually able to do it.

The final assessment for **motor skills** involves ensuring that the learner can successfully perform the movement routine you're teaching, using their own muscles.

Let's say that your course as a whole teaches a how-to skill, such as how to crush the competition by manufacturing widgets at home in your spare time. As you can probably tell from the title, one of the "ingredients" needed to perform this skill is the right attitude. Learners are going to have to be highly motivated to crush the competition. You can monitor and assess how they're doing in adopting this attitude, as part of a support group or membership site.

The course might *also* include a motor skills component, such as teaching efficient hand movements for manufacturing widgets. You can assess (or help learners assess) whether they have mastered the motor skill by having them make a video of their own hand movements and compare it to a demonstration by an expert.

Assessments that take place during a course are called *formative assessments*. They provide learners with feedback as to whether they are on track to achieve the course goal. Are they maintaining the proper attitude? Are they mastering the needed hand movements?

Assessments that take place at the end of a course tell you and your learners whether they have achieved the learning goal for the course as a whole—in this case, crushing the competition by manufacturing widgets at home. You would have to help your learners set up benchmarks and guidelines for how to measure success. For example, "What is the competition doing and how will we crush them?"

Your final assessment for *any* learning activity needs to refer back to the learning goal for that activity, so that you and your learners can know that they have actually learned it.

Event 9: Help Learners Expand on What They've Learned so They May Use It in Other Contexts, Beyond Your Course

You might think that once a student has taken some kind of test to assess what they've learned, the lesson is over. Not so fast.

In order to really cement learning and anchor it to the student's life beyond the classroom or online-learning space, there is an additional step that Gagné observed in the lesson-planning repertoires of excellent teachers.

The ninth step of instruction involves helping students consolidate and expand on what they've learned, by applying this new learning to the broader context of their lives.[8]

If your class involves job-related training, this step would involve the learners applying what they've learned in the performance of their actual jobs.

If you are teaching a language course, this step would involve holding actual conversations with speakers of the target language in a real-world context.

In our imaginary cake-baking class, this step could include an activity such as having the student plan and prepare a cake for an upcoming special occasion at home, school, or work.

If your students have passed the written portion of a driving test, the next step for them is to begin instruction behind the wheel of an actual car.

Once the assessment stage has shown you and your students that they have achieved your course's learning goal, the final step is for them to take their new learning out for a spin under real-world conditions that extend beyond the classroom or online learning space.

This is where you can really get creative with your lesson design.

This also could be the most fun part for you and your learners. After all, your students signed up for your class in order to learn how to do something that matters to them in their actual lives. Here is their chance . . . and your chance to see that not only have they have indeed learned how to do that, but they can now do it independently under realistic conditions.

This is the last step before letting go of the teaching/learning relationship, at least for this specific course. Your learners are taking the training wheels off and actually riding the bike by themselves, so to speak.

If you would like to download a lesson-planning infographic that will help you plan each lesson in your course, go to my website (see "Next Steps").

NINE

....

STEP 5: SELECT YOUR MEDIA
AND BUILD YOUR COURSE

Returning to our house-building metaphor, you've now set up all the rooms (lessons) and determined the function of each. You know the learning goal for each lesson within the larger structure of your course. You've planned each lesson to move your learners closer and closer to the transformation your course promises.

Now the preplanning work you've done is going to pay off by making it fast and easy to actually build your course. The planning process we've been going through is like making a scale model of your furniture and moving everything around on paper before you decide where your physical couch should go.

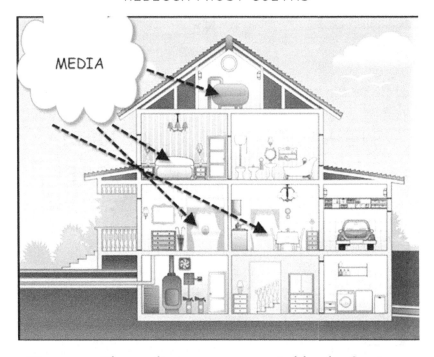

Figure 9.1. The media in your course is like the furniture, décor, and appliances that make a house a home. (Source: Learn and Get Smarter, Inc./Getty Images)

We don't want to go to the trouble of physically dragging a heavy couch up three flights of stairs, only to find out that it won't fit or doesn't look good in the room we are trying to put it in. Similarly, if anything in your course outline doesn't feel clear or right to you at this stage, that's OK! Be happy you didn't waste time creating your media items yet. Keep working on your course outline and lesson plans until everything snaps into place. You'll know when it feels right because your course content will practically jump off the page and into your mind.

Also, test your material out on someone who doesn't have your level of expertise in your subject matter, to be sure it's equally clear to them.

Select Your Media

Once you have planned your lesson content, it is time to select the media you will use to deliver that content. This is like picking out the wallpaper, furniture, and other elements of decor that make a room livable.

Notice that selecting the media you will use to create your content is one of the *last* steps of the Course Design Formula® That's because the affordances and constraints of your course platform and lesson media should not determine how you will set up and build your course. The affordances and constraints of how people learn (which is what the Course Design Formula® helps you focus on) must come first.

Now that you have (correctly) put human learning requirements first, the time has come to select the media you will use to create your lessons. But how do you select them? Select your media based on the lesson's content. Look at the content and ask yourself:

"What is the most effective way to present this specific content to make it easy to learn?"

For example, if your lesson content requires learners to say the days of the week in Spanish, it would be most effective to teach that using an audio file with a native Spanish speaker pronouncing the name of each day correctly. But if your lesson teaches how to slice an onion, a short video demo would be more effective.

Another advantage of planning your content first and then selecting media is that you can be sure to focus your media usage on exactly the content that needs to be taught. Keep your media decisions focused, relevant, and tight. The media is there to deliver the content to the learner's brain, not to be flashy in and of itself.

When you are decorating a room, you want your visitors to say, "What a peaceful and lovely room!" not "What an interesting choice of wallpaper." When you are getting dressed to go out, you want people to say, "You look great!" not "What's going on with your eye makeup?"

Similarly, you want your course participants to be engaged and fascinated by your lesson content, not distracted by the media you're using to deliver it. The media's job is to deliver the content to the learner's brain as unobtrusively as possible. The media should be transparent, so the content is all the learner sees.

Multimedia Design Principles

Educational researcher and theorist Richard E. Mayer identified principles that help learners retain and transfer learning through multimedia resources.[1] He defines *multimedia learning* as "learning from words and pictures."[2] All of his principles are focused on the reduction of cognitive load needed for various kinds of mental information processing.

Mayer identifies *extraneous processing* as mental processing that is not essential to attainment of the learning objective.[3] If the learning material requires extraneous processing, the learner is being asked to work harder than necessary. The material is imposing extraneous cognitive load, which by definition needs to be eliminated.

Mayer uses the term *essential processing* to describe mental work that is essential to achieving the learning objective.[4] He uses the term *generative processing* to describe mental work that helps learners organize new material and integrate it with their prior knowledge.[5] His generative processing aligns with Gagné's ninth event of instruction, enhancing retention and transfer.[6]

Mayer's evidence-based guidelines for designing multimedia instruction include the following:.[7]

To reduce extraneous processing:

- Eliminate extraneous material.
- Highlight essential material.
- Place printed text next to the relevant parts of a graphic.
- Present graphics and the words that describe them at the same time.

To facilitate essential processing:

- Break down narrated animations into learner-paced segments.
- Provide pre-training on the discrete elements of a complex animation.

To encourage generative processing:

- Add appropriate graphics to text.
- Use a conversational rather than formal style.

Some additional multimedia guidelines from Mayer and others[8]:

- Limit the amount of new material presented at any one time.

- Use appropriate graphics with text.
- Avoid extraneous graphics and text.
- Allow the learner to control the pace of instruction.

What does all this mean for you as you select the media for your course? Keep your media focused on exactly what you want your course participants to learn from the content you are presenting. Everything in your course, including its media, must contribute directly to the course learning goal.

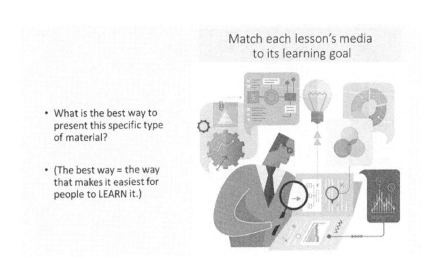

Figure 9.2. Match each lesson's media to its learning goal. (Source: Learn and Get Smarter, Inc./Getty Images)

PART THREE

PREPARE YOUR COURSE
FOR SUCCESS

....

TEN

MAKE YOUR MATERIAL EASY TO UNDERSTAND

Congratulations! You've structured your course, planned your content, and selected the media you will use to build each part of your course. Give yourself a big pat on the back for a job well done. The planning you've put in up front will save you time and trouble as you build your course, because you'll be sure you are creating the right content in the right sequence and using the right media to produce the transformation your course promises. But for your course to be most effective, there are even more factors to consider before you start to build it.

Cognitive load theory helps us optimize our course materials to make them easier to understand. Look over your outline and lesson plans searching for places where the learning doesn't seem to be flowing as well as it could.

Think of the flow of learning as an electrical current and your course as the wires through which that current flows from your mind into your learners' minds. If you set up the wiring (your course structure) correctly, and then pass just the right type and amount of electricity (course content) through that structure in the right sequence and pace, the result is a light-bulb moment where your learners easily understand the new material in an illuminating way.

What can get in the way of these light-bulb moments we all want our students to have?

If there is a kink, twist, or break in the wiring of your course structure—places where there is a lack of continuity, something is suddenly not clear, or you are trying to push too much content through at once—then learners won't be learning. This is analogous to having faulty wiring that doesn't get the electricity to where it needs to go.

Another thing that stops the flow of learning is resistance in the "wire." In this case, the *wires* are the synapses in our brains, which can only process so much information at a time.

If your material has high *intrinsic cognitive load* (it's naturally difficult to understand), then it may be necessary to break it down into smaller chunks that can be processed one at a time. Another way to deal with high intrinsic cognitive load is to make sure your learners have all the prior knowledge they need to process the new information you are teaching them.

It's important to eliminate *extrinsic cognitive load*, as well. If your material is simple but your explanation is confusing, overly complex, or off track, then lightbulb moments are not going to happen either. This is analogous to faulty wiring that doesn't get the electricity to where it needs to go. Scan your course outline and lesson plans looking for places where your explanations may be overly complex or your lesson may be getting off track. Now is the time to catch problems and correct any issues you discover—before you spend time building course content that doesn't do what you want it to.

Finally, *germane cognitive load* measures the learners' engagement level in the learning task. The key here is to optimize engagement, so that your learners focus on the learning material more than on the activity in which it is packaged. In other words, the way you "package" your lesson should be intriguing enough to get your students to open the package, but not *so* intriguing that they spend all their time playing with the packaging while ignoring what's inside the box.

ELEVEN

....

MAKE YOUR LESSONS
MOTIVATING

Students lacking motivation are unlikely to persist in a learning task long enough to overcome the challenges posed by learning something new. For this reason, it's important to build motivational factors directly into your learning design.

Motivation can either come from external sources (such as family pressure or a school, job, or legal requirement), or from internal sources (such as personal interest, the desire to impress someone, or the wish to achieve a personal goal). But motivation in online learning seems to work a bit differently than it does in real-world learning. I discovered this through a series of simultaneous experiences that I had at the dawn of time—relative to online learning—namely, sometime in the late 1990s.

Sit back, relax, and let me tell you a story.

Back when online learning was young, two things happened to me at around the same time. One was that I decided to learn something I'd been fascinated by since the fourth grade: Egyptian hieroglyphics. The other thing that happened around that same time is that I got a speeding ticket. (I've been really good and haven't gotten another one since, I promise.)

I happened to discover an amazing website for learning Egyptian hieroglyphics. The site creator was an accomplished scholar in the field. The site was beautifully organized. The lessons were clear, well designed, and to the point. There was a group of dedicated students who reviewed the lessons in glowing terms. I paid for the course (and it was not cheap). I jumped into the lessons, eager to accomplish my lifelong goal of learning Egyptian hieroglyphics. I discovered that learning Egyptian hieroglyphics is hard. I told myself I would get back to it later. And then . . . I never did.

I found this experience puzzling, because my motivation to learn hieroglyphics (I thought) was high. The course was well designed and actually taught what it was supposed to. And yet when I hit the first barrier to learning, high intrinsic cognitive load (the subject matter is naturally difficult), I ran screaming from the room, and never went back. Needless to say, the experience did not make me proud of myself.

This was not the course designer's fault. She had done a magnificent job of designing the course. Realizing this made me feel even worse about not following through on something I had thought of as an important personal goal.

At the same time, I got that speeding ticket. I had gotten a speeding ticket once before in the distant past, and as a result, had gone to traffic school. The State of California allows drivers with good driving records to go to traffic school in order to learn an important safety lesson and reform their ways, without ending up with a negative mark on their driving record if they can pass a test at the end.

Traffic school is meant to be a wakeup call. It's not meant to be warm, fuzzy, and fun. Back in the old days before the internet, traffic school took place in physical locations. The one I had attended long ago had been up a creaky set of stairs in a building that felt like a fire trap. My fellow traffic school students and I were not the most joyful bunch of schoolmates. None of us was happy to have ended up there, of course. We just wanted to learn our lesson and get it over with. What I remember most from the experience was how uncomfortable the chairs were, how unpleasant the physical environment was, and that the lessons were not fun.

I knew I deserved it, so I took my lumps, passed my test, and was glad to get it over with. And now, many, many years later, I once again found myself in a situation of needing to go to traffic school . . . but this time, there was an option to do it online. Not wanting to climb up another set of creaky stairs to a scary room over a storefront, I jumped at the chance.

To my very great surprise (because I was still struggling with the Egyptian hieroglyphics online lessons), the online traffic school lessons were fabulous! I absolutely loved them. Like the Egyptian lessons, the traffic school lessons were clear and well designed. Like the Egyptian lessons, the traffic school lessons focused clearly on the learning goal. But unlike the Egyptian lessons, which were on a subject where my internal motivation to learn was high, I did not run screaming from the room during online traffic school.

The difference was the source of the motivation. There was a strong external motivation to complete the online traffic school lessons, because the alternatives were either a return to the creaky room over the storefront or a ding on my driving record.

It's not surprising that I completed the lessons. But what is surprising—or was to me, at that time—was that I actually enjoyed them. I was motivated to complete them not only by the high cost of auto insurance and the long arm of the law, but also by the sheer love of learning online.

Why? I kept asking myself. Why did I so much enjoy the online traffic school lessons, and not the online hieroglyphic lessons? This seemed counterintuitive, to say the least. I thought about it a lot and eventually came up with the answer. The reasons are complex, so let's dive into them and see what we can learn about learner motivation to complete an online course.

Three Factors to Consider That Motivate Online Learners

Here are three considerations that motivate learners to join and complete online courses.

1. **When considering a learner's motivation for online learning, it's important to recognize what other options they have for learning the same material.** My other options for learning hieroglyphics would have been to take a dream-of-a-lifetime trip to

Egypt, visit fascinating archeological sites, and take classes in comfortable classrooms filled with interesting strangers. Since I enjoy foreign travel, archaeological sites, and meeting interesting people, that would have been a lot more appealing than taking any online class, no matter how well designed.

Granted, I had no plans to travel to Egypt to study hieroglyphics. It's just that I realized I could. In fact, the online class I was taking showed pictures and videos of other people, including the instructor, who were doing just that. It was clear from those pictures that they were having a lot of fun. I, however, was not. My vicarious engagement in the task of learning hieroglyphics could not possibly match what I was seeing others doing in real life, on the screen.

By contrast, my other option for completing traffic school was to spend hours in an unpleasant physical environment with a cohort of unhappy strangers. Just by being able to study the traffic school material online and not in the real world, I already felt very lucky. I was happy to be in the online class because the alternative was a lot worse.

2. **When considering a learner's motivation for online learning, consider how important and how urgent the learning goal is to them.** In *The 7 Habits of Highly Effective People*, Stephen R. Covey shares the Eisenhower decision matrix, a system of four quadrants to help prioritize goals and tasks.[1] The four options are urgent/important, urgent/not important, not urgent/important, and not urgent/not important.

Plugging these two course topics into that matrix shows us something revealing: completing online traffic school was both important and urgent. I had to finish the online course by a specific deadline to keep a dreaded black mark off my driving record.

Learning hieroglyphics, on the other hand, was not urgent. Hieroglyphics have been around for 5,000 years and they are not going anywhere. But more surprising (at least to me, since I'd been fascinated by the topic since I was nine years old), learning hieroglyphics was also not important—at least, not to me.

How can that be? I was motivated because I wanted to do it. I was interested. The subject matter was pleasant—or would have been if it were not so hard.

It was pleasant to think about. If knowledge of Egyptian hieroglyphics were a skill that could have fallen into my brain by osmosis, without any effort on my part, I would have been delighted. But once the opportunity was presented to me (by the easy availability of online learning, requiring no trip to Egypt and no effort to look attractive for interesting strangers), *boom*, it all fell apart.

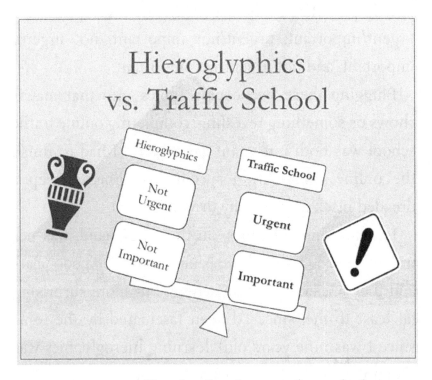

Figure 11.1. Traffic school vs. learning hieroglyphics, plugged into the Eisenhower matrix. (Source: Learn and Get Smarter, Inc.)

Remember, there was no external motivation for me to complete the hieroglyphics course. I didn't need it for a university grade, an upcoming job, or a planned archaeological adventure. If the situation could have been summed up by a mathematical equation, it would have looked something like this.

Internal motivation + external motivation + germane cognitive load **must be GREATER THAN** *intrinsic cognitive load + extraneous cognitive load*

Internal motivation is made up of[2]:

- Curiosity.
- Self-efficacy.
- Achievement.

So, each of those three things, considered on its own merits, is only a third of the internal motivation any individual learner may have to learn something. In my case, my curiosity about learning hieroglyphics was high. But as it turns out, curiosity only counts for a third of the internal motivation factors a learner must have in order to be 100 percent internally motivated to learn something.

Let's compare the two sides of the equation. (The math isn't real. I'm just making this up to illustrate a point.)

On a scale of 1–100 (with 100 being best), my internal motivation for learning hieroglyphics was 33.3 (33.3 for curiosity, 0 for self-efficacy, 0 for achievement).

My external motivation was zero. And my involvement in the learning (germane cognitive load) was pretty low, too, especially compared to taking a trip to Egypt surrounded by interesting strangers. So, neither external motivation nor germane cognitive load contributed much to my "score," let's say 20 points.

Now for the other side of the equation. Intrinsic cognitive load (the difficulty in learning that is a natural part of the subject matter) was high, let's say, 90. Extraneous cognitive load (imposed by the online learning interface itself, rather than poor course design in this case), was about 50.

So, we have: 33.3 + 0 + 20 on the motivation and engagement side of the equation (the left), and 90 + 50 on the learning difficulty side (the right). A motivation/engagement score of 55.3 is *not* greater than a learning difficulty score of 140, which is why I gave up and didn't complete the course.

I was highly interested in the subject matter, but that was not enough by itself to compensate for the other factors involved.

Now let's "do the math" for traffic school.

Internal motivation = 66.6

- Curiosity: 0
- Self-efficacy: 33.3
- Achievement 33.3

External motivation: 100 (I did not want a mark on my driving record).

Intrinsic cognitive load: 0 (this stuff is easy).

Extrinsic cognitive load: 0 (the lessons were well designed and worked well in an online format because I got immediate feedback that I'd gotten answers right).

Germane cognitive load: 50 (the lessons were well designed and actually interesting, and I felt a sense of engagement by getting answers right and moving closer to my goal).

So we have a score of (66.6 + 100 + 50 = 216.6) for motivation and engagement, which is much greater than the score of 0 (zero) difficulty in learning the material.

When we add up the various factors involved, it becomes clear why I finished the traffic school course (and even felt good about it) but gave up on hieroglyphics. Curiosity about the subject matter is an important factor, but it's only one of many.

For the hieroglyphics course, my internal motivation was not strong enough to overcome the resistance posed by the subject matter's intrinsic cognitive load. Although the course designer did a great job of reducing cognitive load as low as it could go, she couldn't take all the difficulty out of the subject matter. When she made it as easy as possible for me to learn this, what I was forced to confront was the realization that it still wasn't easy enough, because I just was not motivated *enough* to overcome the learning challenges posed by the subject matter itself.

The subject was interesting to me. But it was not critical. Nothing in my life depended on it. It was not important. Other priorities, such as completing online traffic school, kept coming first.

What does this tell you as an online course designer? It tells you that no matter how well you design your course, and how many students you sign up because they are motivated and interested in learning the subject matter, **you will see a higher rate of course completion if the topic is both urgent and important to your learners.** In other words, before you spend a lot of time preparing even the tastiest well-seasoned food, be sure people are actually hungry enough to eat it.

For the most part, this topic falls into the area of digital marketing, more than the area of instructional design. But there is an instructional-design aspect that is appropriate to focus on, which is designing your course in a way that not only appeals to, but also motivates your learners. Let's look at that next.

3. **When considering learner motivation, consider how much time and effort it will take before learners experience achievement and rewards from taking your course.** Three factors that Gagné identifies as important for keeping learners motivated are curiosity, self-efficacy, and achievement.[3] Continuing with our hieroglyphics/traffic school example, we can see that while curiosity was an important factor in getting me to sign up and pay for the hieroglyphics course, it was not enough to make me stick with it once the going got tough.

On the other hand, curiosity played little to no role in my signing up for online traffic school. The motivation to take the course came from external factors. But once I got started with the traffic school lessons, I did, in fact, find it motivating to continue them, regardless of those external factors. The traffic class was motivating because every time I performed a short learning activity, I had to check something off or take a short quiz. I could see the results of my progress through the required program, clearly and easily.

Every time I checked something off, I was that much closer to completing the requirement that had led me to take the course. Even though the subject matter was not motivating in and of itself, the feeling of getting closer and closer to an important goal in a clearly observable manner was. That felt good.

The traffic school course made me feel like a success because as long as I read the material it was easy to answer the questions, do well on the quiz, and make my life immediately better by moving closer to solving an important and urgent matter. It was possible to complete the entire course in about three days. Working on the course each of those days gave me a strong feeling of achievement and self-efficacy as I moved closer to solving an urgent and important problem, day by day.

The hieroglyphics course, on the other hand, didn't help me solve a problem. Instead, it showed me that I *had* a problem. My problem was that, unlike other students whose progress I could see in the class, I was not finding learning hieroglyphics easy. This was shocking and surprising to me because I am generally very good at learning languages, and because I had wanted to learn hieroglyphics since I was a child.

The hieroglyphics course was well designed from an instructional design point of view, and other students seemed to be learning a lot from it, so I am guessing the problem was with me. I am spatially challenged, so perhaps languages (such as hieroglyphics and sign language) that have a strong spatial component may be harder for me to learn than more purely phonetically based languages.

For whatever reason, the more I delved into the hieroglyphics online course material, the more I could see that I was not good at learning this subject matter. That feeling was the opposite of achievement and self-efficacy. I felt that I was not an effective learner and I was not making progress toward my intended learning goal. And since achieving the goal was neither urgent nor important, the simplest and most effective response was to simply stop engaging with the course material, even though I had already paid for it.

Now, if that same course had been a requirement for a university-level degree program in ancient languages, or if I had needed to pass it in order to get certified for an archaeology job I was applying for, there would have been an external motivation to continue past any difficulty. I could have contacted the instructor or gotten additional help. But I didn't because I was not motivated enough to do so.

I had paid for the course because I wanted to learn something that was enjoyable to me. When I discovered that I wasn't learning and it wasn't enjoyable, I just stopped doing it.

How This Information Applies to Your Online Course

There might be any number of students like me, taking your or any instructor's online course. No matter how hard you try, you won't be able to meet the needs of every student. The designer of that hieroglyphics course did nothing wrong. I thought her course was exemplary. I just find it interesting that even a generally hard working student who is motivated to take an online course, may not persist for reasons the course designer can't control. But perhaps we can learn some things from what worked in the traffic school course that could apply to other courses (like the hieroglyphics one)—or to your future courses as you think about how to design them for maximum learner motivation and engagement.

The most important difference I see between my experience of the traffic school course and my experience of the hieroglyphics course is that in the traffic school course I got immediate rewards. Every time I logged on and paid attention to a lesson, I got feedback that I had learned what I was supposed to learn, and I could check something off on a timeline that clearly moved me closer to my goal. I could achieve my goal in a short amount of time. I could move myself closer to a desirable result, via my own efforts. And those efforts involved logging in to the course every day and doing what it said, until done. Also, all of this was quite easy.

The hieroglyphics course on the other hand showed me a vast panorama of future potential—all of which seemed difficult and out of reach. I could see other students reading and writing in hieroglyphics. I could see people going on field trips to Egypt. I could see that I was not getting everything in even the beginning lessons, and that it was going to take a lot of lessons (in which I was already not doing a fantastic job) to reach my learning goals. Every time I logged on, I felt like more of a failure at achieving my own goals—goals that I wanted to achieve and had paid good money for. That wasn't a good feeling at all.

What can we learn from this in designing our own online courses? Clearly, **if your course solves an urgent** and important issue in your students' lives, they will be more motivated to complete it than if it does not. But any issue is going to be urgent and important to some people, while not to others.

The most important lesson I take away from this is that **we should design our courses in ways that *ensure* learners will be successful *every* step of the way,** and provide learners with a clear path of progress to achieving the course goal.

Also, it makes more sense to design our courses in relatively small increments, even if we are covering a giant topic. For example, what if in the hieroglyphics course, the goal had only been to teach me how to read one word, or to write my own name? That would have been simple and relatively easy to achieve. I would have felt a sense of accomplishment and achievement.

True, I would have been far from the long-term goal of actually reading hieroglyphics, but I would have already achieved the short-term goal of successfully reading one word. Instead of being turned off to the subject because it felt too overwhelming, I would have been motivated to keep going and learn more.

As an independent online course creator, you probably don't have access to the types of external motivators that ensure people finish a course in an academic or corporate training setting (or at traffic school). Your course probably doesn't deliver grades or impose penalties for non-completion. Your course is more likely part of the curriculum in the School of Life, and your goal is to help your learners improve their lives in ways that matter to them.

But self-improvement, even if it matters to us, is hard. Real learning requires effort and actually changes our brains. And it's only natural that people resist change— even changes they've signed up for, paid for, and sincerely want to make, as my hieroglyphics course experience shows.

In order to overcome these challenges, you will need to build factors that support and enhance internal motivation into every aspect of your course. In addition to identifying curiosity, self-efficacy, and achievement as factors that increase learner motivation, Gagné also further elaborated on the ARCS model of motivational factors originally developed by J.M. Keller. The acronym ARCS is short for attention, relevance, confidence, and satisfaction.[4] Gagné's recommendations based on that model include[5]:

- **Hold learners' attention** by varying the format you use for presenting the material.

- **Help learners grasp complex abstract ideas** by using concrete examples and analogies.
- **Provoke curiosity** with paradox, surprise, conflict, humor, incongruities, and jokes.[6]

Here are some ways, based on the ARCS model, that you can build motivating factors into your course, modules, and lessons.[7]

To gain attention:

- Use varying formats.
- Make abstract ideas clear and easy to grasp.
- Incorporate humor, paradox, and surprise.

To ensure relevance:

- Relate the lesson material to students' prior knowledge.
- Clarify the immediate usefulness of learning the material.
- Explain how learning this material will benefit learners in the future.

To enhance learner confidence:

- Present clear, skills-based learning objectives.
- Sequence learning tasks in small segments.
- Allow the learner to achieve success at each step.

- Allow learners to control lesson sequence and pace.

To ensure learner **satisfaction**:
- Provide performance-based feedback at every step of the learning sequence.
- Help students generalize the learning to a larger context beyond the immediate lesson.

Group related material in meaningful chunks to make it easier for students to process and remember.[8] Allow students to organize newly learned material mentally in personally meaningful ways.[9]

Keep these motivating factors in mind as you design your course. Ask yourself, *How can I make learners curious about what's coming next? How can I encourage them to take effective action on their own behalf, rather than just absorbing the course material passively? How can I build a strong learner achievement component into my lessons?*

If your course involves a large amount of subject matter, or has high intrinsic cognitive load, you might consider breaking it down into a series of bite-sized mini-courses (or mini-modules, or mini-lessons) so that your students can get a sense of achievement and progress for completing something relatively quickly.

It's critical to keep that sense of achievement and forward progress going in your online course, every step of the way. If you lose it at any point, your learners may give up and never come back.

As you think about the courses you want to create and how you want to structure them, keep the idea of making each course smaller in mind. Give students a feeling of rapid accomplishment and clear success in reaching a specific goal, right from the beginning. That way you will keep them coming back for more.

Figure 11.2. Build motivational factors into your lessons. (Source: Learn and Get Smarter, Inc./Getty Images)

···

TWELVE

MAKE YOUR LEARNER THE FOCUS AS YOU DESIGN AND BUILD YOUR COURSE

In this chapter, we will explore how you can set up your course to support your learners emotionally and socially, so that you create a class environment conducive to learning. Then we will look at ways to build cognitive and intellectual support structures into your course as well.

Learner-Centered Design

In our excitement to create online courses, it's important to remember what's on the other side of the screen: a human being who wants to learn something. There are many "cheat sheets" and guides to creating online courses that provide excellent information about the technology side of the equation—how to set up your website, how to record video, and so on—but make no mention at all of how to actually teach human beings.

It's important to learn how to use the technology, of course, but it's even more important to understand how your course participants will interact with and learn from the online course materials you create—and what you must do to ensure that they learn from them.

Even if you are an experienced teacher in face-to-face settings, teaching online is different. Teaching online requires you to manage cognitive load differently than you would in a physical classroom and brings in a different set of affordances and constraints. Keeping track of all that, plus technology and media, is not easy, but that doesn't excuse us from remembering that there's a real person sitting on the other side of that screen: a real person who wants to learn something from us.

Design for the Learner as a Multifaceted Person

Understanding learners' needs is the most challenging aspect of delivering effective teaching in an online context.

When you teach in a face-to-face setting, you get constant, immediate feedback as to whether or not you are meeting your learners' needs. If the room is too cold, everyone starts shivering. If there are not enough chairs, you see people standing in the back of the lecture hall or sitting on the floor. If the class is not holding their attention, you see your students fidgeting, doodling, passing notes, texting, or falling asleep.

In an online setting, it is harder to see these things, yet we must still account for them.

As human beings, we exist in multiple dimensions: physical, emotional, social, intellectual, aspirational, and spiritual. Although online learning mainly engages your learners' minds, the other dimensions of their being are also present while they are interacting with your course. If your course is not engaging them on the social and emotional levels (and sometimes even if it is), your learners may meet their social and emotional needs by talking to their friends on social media while "studying" your lesson material.

(Admit it, we've all done that ourselves, too).

If your course asks them to use their eyes by watching a video, but it turns out the video is just a talking head, they are going to open another tab and move their eyes over to another website while treating your "video" as an audio file playing in the background.

Many adult learners lead extremely busy lives. They're working full time, commuting, trying to find time for exercise, and juggling housework and childcare. If your course is set up in a way that requires them to sit still looking at a screen for long periods of time, you are holding their physical bodies hostage, making it impossible for them to do anything else at the same time (or pushing them to do other screen-related tasks at the same time as yours, because of the limited screen time they have).

It takes a lot of dedication, persistence, and hard work to create an online course. Your needs as a course creator are important too. If you've put in the time, effort, and expense to create a series of videos for your course, you certainly want to be sure that your students are going to watch them. This is especially important if video is the main or only lesson delivery medium your course has—if video *is* your course.

Instead of automatically using video as a teaching tool, first analyze the lesson content and then select your media based on the most efficient way to convey that content. Use simpler, rather than more complex types of media in order to reduce extraneous cognitive load.

I realize that may sound counter intuitive. I mean, don't we need more fancy multimedia bells and whistles to make our online learning pop?

No, we don't.

We need clearly focused, tightly designed lessons that properly balance cognitive load, while taking the learner as a whole person with varying goals, motivations, and needs into account.

As an online instructor, you have an opportunity that classroom teachers don't: you have the ability to direct your learners' sensory attention exactly where you want it to go. But you only get to use this power for a minute. Your ability to direct your learners' attention where you want it to go is greatest at the very beginning of your course and at the very beginning of each lesson. If your learners quickly see that your focus is not sharp, clear, and precise, and that you have directed their attention somewhere it does not really have to be, they will take matters back into their own hands and direct their own attention wherever *they* want it to go. You will have lost the authority you had (for a minute) to direct their focus.

Just as a classroom teacher will quickly lose control of the class if he or she does not understand the basic principles of classroom management, so will you, as an online teacher, soon find your students surfing the web, chatting on social media, and leaving the room entirely to get a snack, unless you grab their attention right from the beginning and focus it exactly where it needs to be to ensure they learn the material.

You cannot achieve this objective merely by telling your students to close down other tabs, turn off their phones, or similar instructions. (You can and perhaps should do that. But simply telling them to focus where you want them to doesn't ensure they will do so.) Your lesson material must grab their attention and hold it.

What ensures their focus on what you want them to focus on is your knowledge of the subject matter, your understanding of and respect for their needs, and your use of instructional design best practices (which you are learning here) to direct attention to exactly where it needs to go through your skillful and appropriate use of online media.

Part of being a teacher, in any context, is establishing authority. If you want your learners to pay attention, you have to show them that what you have to offer *deserves* their full attention. If you are trying to teach us about electric current by showing us a video of you talking to us, our attention is focused on your face. There is no electric current on your face. (At least, I sincerely hope there isn't!) Your face cannot help your students learn about electric current, therefore showing us your face is not a good use of the capacity of online media to direct our attention exactly where you want it to go.

What do you want your learners' attention to be focused on? Electric current. So, what do you need to be showing them? A video that directly demonstrates live electric current.

It's as simple as that.

"But wait!" you may say. "Before I show them the video about electric current, I need to explain a few things. I need to talk to them."

Fair enough. What's the best way for your learners to focus on you talking to them? By listening to your voice.

What's the best online medium to use for listening to your voice? An audio file.

Learners can listen to an audio file while their eyes are focused elsewhere. If the audio file contains a general introduction that is not too complex, they can do household chores like washing the dishes or folding clothes, or do exercises such as aerobics or running, while listening. For some people, performing physical activity (of a type that does not require a lot of concentration) actually helps to enhance their mental focus while listening.

If you need to introduce yourself as an authority on your topic and explain who you are and how you know what you are about to share, then *you* are the subject matter. In that case, it is not only appropriate, it's essential, to focus the video on yourself talking to the students—but only up to the part of the lesson where you start teaching about electric current (or whatever else your lesson content involves). Use your lesson media to focus the learner's attention directly on the exact subject matter for each part of your lesson.

You show consideration for your learners' busy schedules and complicated lives by not holding their muscles and visual systems hostage for extended periods of time—unless the specific demands of the subject matter dictate that you absolutely must.

For presenting verbal information, slides often are more appropriate than video. Slides allow you to fulfill the criteria Gagné found important for teaching verbal information[1]:

- Present small amounts of text or audio narration at a time.
- Add relevant graphics that provide context for the words.

- Allow the learner to control the pace of instruction.

If you are presenting verbal information, keep in mind that video goes by too fast to allow the learner to control the pace of instruction, but slides are perfect for this. Slides do not have to be monotonous or boring. You can present slides in many formats.

Here are just a few examples of how you can present slides in an online course (for more ideas, see "Resources"). You could use:

- PowerPoint presentations.
- Digital flipbooks.
- Downloadable PDFs.
- Digital flashcards, using an app like Quizlet.
- Programs, such as VoiceThread, that allow for group discussions of each slide.

Video should be used when its affordances are relevant to the learning content. For example, video is ideal for demonstrating anything that needs to be seen as part of a movement sequence, for taking students to remote locations, for understanding complex ideas that are best portrayed in a visually sequential format, and so on.

Audio should be used when students need to hear your words while doing something else. For example, an audio file would be a great way to walk learners through the steps of a recipe that they need actually to cook in the kitchen, or through a movement routine that they need to perform outdoors.

In order to help your students make best use of their time, it is thoughtful and considerate to include a note about the playing time of audio and video files at the beginning of each lesson.

If your student is folding clothes while listening to your audio, they are not on social media and they are not surfing other websites, activities that would distract them from what you are saying. Your lesson will be more effective and also more considerate of your learners' time.

What if the material you are talking about is complex, and has high intrinsic cognitive load? In that case, it is helpful to provide a printable text version highlighting the important points.

Alternatively, if you want the student to listen and create the text version themselves, you could require them to take notes on their tablet or smartphone while listening to you speak.

If you cut learners some slack when it doesn't really matter (for example, by making it easy for them to do tasks like fold the laundry while listening to your MP3 file for twenty minutes), they will more easily give you their full attention when it is truly required. Your respect for their time will generate an equal and opposite respect for the time you put into creating your multimedia lesson materials. This type of respect for and understanding of your students' needs is an aspect of your care for them and an embodiment of your practice of transformative teaching in an online context.

Design for Individual Differences

Each of us is a unique individual. We each learn best in our own way.

Learning styles have been defined and classified in various ways.[2] One popular viewpoint says there are four learning styles: visual, auditory, tactile, and kinesthetic.[3] Other classification systems include learning styles relating to whether someone learns best alone or in a group, and whether logically or intuitively, among other factors.[4]

How can we account for these sorts of differences when designing an online course that has to serve many different learners' needs? One way is to build flexibility and options into your course, especially in terms of how learners access the material.

Now let's back up a minute. After all, you, the course designer, are an individual too. You are working hard to design your course. It's no easy feat to design a lesson to be accessed in one way—for example, by watching a video. Am I really saying that once you've gone to all the trouble of designing your lesson in one format, you then have to go back and design it in several other formats, too? Isn't that a bit like having to cook five different dinners because everyone in the family has specific food preferences and tastes?

Well, yes and no.

Your biggest challenge in creating your course is to get it created to begin with. You have individual differences too. You are just as unique as everybody else. Your teaching style is just as important as your learners' learning styles. Maybe more so, since you are the one making the entire course happen to begin with.

So, if you love creating videos and hate writing, I am not telling you to ditch the video and write your course as a series of written lessons, the first time around. If the idea of doing that would kill your creative process and stop your course production in its tracks, for goodness sake don't go there. Just get it done, whatever way works best for you.

But then there's the ongoing process of course revision. Once you have the basic format of your course designed, and you have your lessons laid out in some tangible medium that students can access, consider this: the more options you give your students for accessing the material, the more you allow them to learn best according to their individual differences.

Keeping different learning styles in mind as you update and revise your course materials will lead to more happy students, and that will lead to more people recommending your course to their friends and signing up for your next course. Ideally, it will become second nature for you to create a transcript of every video you make and also save it as an audio file for MP3 playback.

I give you permission not to be perfect (I'm not!). I have not had a chance to do all of this yet for all of my own courses, either. This is a long term goal to aim for, but don't let it get in the way of getting started sharing your expertise.

Now, some lessons lend themselves to being taught in one multimedia format and not another. In that case, think about different aspects of the lesson as a whole that could still be presented in different formats to accommodate multiple learning styles.

For example, let's say one of your lessons features a video demonstration of how to bake a pie. It's important for students to watch you actually making the pie. Demonstrating that is what video does well.

But in order to make the pie by themselves, it would help students to have a downloadable printed shopping list and a downloadable printed recipe, as well as an audio version of you reading the instructions out loud so they can listen to the instructions while they are in the kitchen making the pie and their hands are covered in flour or occupied with tasks like rolling crust.

There are three important questions to consider when it comes to designing e-learning for different learning styles.

1. **What is the best way to present the material itself?** This is the primary and most important factor in how to present your course content, learning styles notwithstanding.[5] If the material needs to be shown visually in order to be understood, then video is the best medium for it.

    Some learners may not be visual learners. They may learn best by listening without involving the visual system (this also goes for students with no or limited sight, which we will talk about when we discuss making your course accessible for learners with various needs). Some learners may prefer reading to watching a video. But if video is the best way to present the material, it makes most sense for the course designer to focus on creating the instruction in a video format to start.

Once the lesson is designed, then an audio-only file and a text-only transcript or narration can be added to assist those who learn best by hearing or reading words.

2. **What is the best way for you, as the course designer, to present the material?** The best way for you to create the material may be a function of your own learning style, or of the materials and resources available to you.

Considering my emphasis on student-centered learning, you might find it strange that I am saying the instructor should put his or her own preference first when creating the course. My reasoning is simple: the only course no one will ever learn from is the course you don't create. So, create it first in whatever way is easiest for you. Then add in other ways for your students to interact with your already-created lessons, later.

3. **What is the best way to create the course, given the online platform you are using?** It's important not to get too attached to whatever online platform you are using, because later you might decide to move your course to a different one. Your course should be defined and shaped by its instructional design, not by the course platform. But that said, it will be easier to design your course if you work with the demands of the platform you're using, rather than fighting them.

   A lot of course platforms are heavily focused on video. That's OK, as long as you don't fall into the trap of thinking that video is the only way to present a lesson in an online course. Even if your chosen course platform leans heavily towards video, it should provide you with other ways to present material to your students as well.

   How can you design the course to allow for individual learning differences? You can make your course come alive for your students by using different learning styles throughout your course based on the most effective way to present each piece of content. This fits well with Gagné's recommendation to increase learner motivation and engagement by adding elements of variety and surprise throughout your course.[6]

Different Ways of Approaching Learning: Right Brain/Left Brain

One of the biggest differences I observe among my course participants is between those who take a generally "left-brained" vs. "right-brained" approach to learning. (I am basing these observations not on scientific research but on direct observation of how my online students experience my course.) In all my years of teaching in physical spaces, I never gave much thought to the left brain/right brain discussion as a factor in curriculum creation. The issue never really came up. But in teaching online it came up constantly as I observed how different students accessed and proceeded through the course material.

(I am using the terms *left-brained* and *right-brained* in the popular sense; the way people use these terms to describe themselves as either predominantly reasoning or feeling in their thought processes. I have not conducted any kind of scientific tests to determine whether people really use one side of their brains more than the other.)

The "left-brained" learners took a direct, sequential approach to the course material. They went through the lessons methodically, one at a time. They completed all the assignments. Their questions focused on practical aspects of the course material. They wanted to get it done, get it done quickly, and get it done correctly. Challenges they experienced related to getting ahead of themselves by trying to put things into practice before fully grasping the big picture, and not understanding how specific parts of the instruction related to the whole.

The "right-brained" learners took a holistic approach to the course material. They were more interested in understanding the big picture than in completing lesson activities in a sequential manner. They got a lot out of participating in group sharing aspects of class discussion. Some of the right-brained learners waited until all of the class meetings were over before beginning to work through the lessons on their own. Challenges they experienced related to taking a long time to get started because they felt they needed the whole perspective before being able to begin. They also sometimes had trouble restricting themselves to a specific course topic, because they saw everything as important and as connected to everything else.

A potential challenge I could see for learners who approach an online course this way is that the rest of the group may have moved on and they'll be left behind in group discussions. One way to proactively account for that possibility is to have an ongoing membership community that all of your course participants (who want to) can be part of. That way, those who take longer to get started on the course activities can get support from other class members, and from you, as the instructor, when they need it.

A membership community will also help the left-brained learners begin to see how all the individual steps of the learning journey you've taken them on fit together to create a cohesive whole.

How can you accommodate both types of learners in your online course? If your course includes live class meetings (for example, on a video conferencing platform like Zoom), you can accommodate both types of learners by using a method that I've found works well.[7] First, go over the week's lesson materials in a systematic, sequential way. Then, open up the discussion for questions and answers, individual sharing, and group support. If you post a replay of the live class, divide it into two separate sections, or let learners know the precise minute (using a time stamp) when the formal lesson ends, and the group discussion begins. That way individual learners can focus on the parts of the lesson that are most personally useful and meaningful to them.

Different Ways of Accessing Information: Learning Modalities

Let's explore the instructional design implications of different learning modalities, which are different sensory pathways for taking in and processing information.

Visual

When you think of teaching online in a visual way, expand your thinking beyond just video. Multimedia best practices suggest that still images work better than quick-moving video images, because they allow students to focus on the information long enough to process and remember it.[8] Unlike video, still images allow the learner to control the pace of instruction.

You can use this principle to design still images that convey the information you are teaching in visual ways. You also can encourage students to observe things in their actual physical environments visually. And you can have them read text. In addition, you can provide them with links to websites where they can observe and learn visually.

There are many ways that people can learn visually. Including more than one method will add variety, expertise, and polish to your course and keep your students focused, interacting, and engaged.

Before adding a visual image to your course—or anything else you did not create yourself, including audios, videos, and text—, be sure you have the legal right to do so. Just because an image (or anything else) is on the internet does not mean it is available for use. All creative materials should be considered copyrighted and available to you only with specific permission from the copyright holder. Unless explicitly stated otherwise, images posted on the internet cannot be used without attribution or licensing.

To find images for use in your course materials, you can search for sites that provide images specifically for commercial use without attribution. Sites such as Pixabay, Unsplash and Wikimedia Commons may have images you can use (see resources), but it is important to read, save, and (of course!) comply with the license that accompanies each image, because usage allowances vary.

If you need to use a lot of images in your course materials, you can buy a licensed image subscription from a site like iStock Photo or Getty Images. These are not cheap, and it is important to be aware of and adhere to the terms of your license, both in general and with respect to what you are allowed to do with any particular image.

Bottom line: make sure you have the legal right to use an image in your course materials *before* you start using it to create any media items.

Auditory

Audio files will clearly appeal to students who learn best by listening. But auditory learning in an online context is more complex than that, because e-learning produces a change in the way sensory preferences intersect with the subject matter.

Even students who are generally visual learners, for example, will prefer audio lessons if the only time they have to focus on your course material is during their daily commute or while working out or doing household chores. They may be visual learners on a personal level, but they become de facto auditory learners on a logistical level if their visual systems are being used for other things while they're accessing your course materials.

There are two important principles to keep in mind: your course will be richer for all your students and will especially appeal to those who are auditory learners, if you include material that allows your students to learn through listening. At the same time, it's important to be sure that any enrichment materials you include in your course that you did not create yourself do not violate anyone else's copyright. You do not want to run afoul of copyright issues in the music industry, for example.

Even if your lessons primarily rely on visual or written material, it is important to provide an audio version for learners who are unable to see. We will talk more about this in the section on making your course accessible for learners with special needs.

Tactile

Tactile learners learn best through touching and getting their hands on objects directly.

You might think that tactile learning is not available in an online learning situation, but that doesn't have to be the case. For example, imagine a lesson about tree identification. Via the online learning interface, the instructor can do all the obvious things, such as show visually what the leaves of each kind of tree look like. But there is no reason the online learning interface can't also instruct students in what the tree's bark texture feels like, up to and including having students go outdoors and find examples of trees in the real world, actually touch their bark, and report back on what the experience was like.

Here's another example: What if the lesson was how to help children with special needs identify letters of the alphabet, and the goal was to help special education teachers come up with creative ways to help their students experience the letters using multiple sensory modalities?

The online lesson could direct the special education teachers to try creative activities such as lining or filling alphabet-shaped cake molds with materials of various textures, ranging from marbles to playdough to sandpaper. And then it could direct the special education teachers to close their eyes and imagine the feel of various textures filling the letter-shaped molds to gain an understanding of what this tactile experience would feel like to their students.

These are just examples, of course. The specific type of tactile activities you include in your own course, if any, would depend on the actual lesson content of your course.

You can think both outside the box and beyond the screen in deciding how to design your lessons.

When you are thinking outside the box about your lessons, remember that in face-to-face learning, teachers sometimes take the class on excursions beyond the classroom walls. Whether just down the hall to the science lab or out into the world to explore a nature preserve, face-to-face learning extends beyond the walls of the physical classroom.

Your online course can expand the possibilities for sensory interaction beyond the screen "walls" of the online classroom, too. Many learners would be glad to engage with a lesson on a mobile device, such as a tablet, a laptop, or—even more portable—a smartphone. Museums have been using this kind of program for years to guide visitors through their galleries. All your students would need, most likely, is a set of headphones (which they probably already have, anyway). With you as their guide or on their own, as a kind of field trip, your students can experience multisensory learning beyond edge of the computer screen.

You could direct your students to engage in an activity with tactile components, such as coloring in a downloadable PDF or infographic that reinforces the content of your video or audio materials.

If your learners are busy coloring while they are listening to your lesson via audio or watching your video, then their hands will not be free to text friends on social media or navigate away to other sites while your course video plays in the background. Just saying.

Kinesthetic

Kinesthetic learning revolves around movement and involves the whole body. When face to face in a classroom, getting students up out of their seats and moving is one way to wake the class up when learners' attention starts to fade. One of the great things about kinesthetic learning is that it tends to involve high germane cognitive load because we have to pay full attention and be fully present when our bodies are moving through space.

Kinesthetic activities get the muscles working and the blood flowing, increase oxygen flow to the brain, and stretch muscles that have tightened from too much sitting.

They also tend to be fun!

Sometimes, the subject matter of an online course inherently promotes kinesthetic learning. If your online course is about how to improve your tennis swing, or how to do the rhumba, then kinesthetic learning is going to be included by default.

You may demonstrate a movement or a dance step and then have students get up and copy what you're showing them how to do on screen, in their own physical space in the real world, for example.

It's harder—though not impossible, if you get creative—to include kinesthetic learning activities in a lesson focused on delivering verbal information, or if you are teaching skills that don't naturally involve movement. But experts say that it is unhealthy to sit in one position for long periods of time.[9] And student attention starts to fade after too much sitting.

It's good when learning to get up and move every fifteen minutes or so. If your lessons consist of short segments, such as videos that take less than fifteen minutes to play, you don't really need to design kinesthetic activities into the lesson. Just by the nature of the online learning experience, students will naturally get up and move around the physical space they are in once the video is over. (They are free to do so at any time, of course. How could you stop them, even if you wanted to?)

Consider the kinesthetic aspects of what your lesson design is asking students to do if you include a video that is forty-five minutes to an hour long. One suggestion would be for students to watch the video while engaged in a (safe) movement activity, such as riding a stationary bike. But most students will not have access to both your course materials and a stationary bike, at the same time.

So, ask yourself if you could break the long video down into several shorter ones, with a natural break after each segment. The natural break could include a comprehension check, and an opportunity to practice or act out some aspect of the lesson material.

If you can include movement in these practice sessions, you are more likely to both sustain the learners' attention during the lesson and help them remember what was learned after the lesson is over.

In Part One, we discussed the narrow focus of short-term memory. It only allows learners to hold on to a few ideas at a time. Presenting a small amount of new material at a time in a series of short videos, will lead to better retention of the material than would presenting an hour's worth of information all at once in one long video.

Adding movement in the form of kinesthetic learning activities will help students promote long-term memory storage of the new information by increasing their alertness and optimizing germane cognitive load. Adding movement activities to your lessons, when appropriate, will also make your lessons more enjoyable and engaging.

See the "Resources" section at the end of this book for links to websites that help promote kinesthetic learning in online courses.

If you do include movement in your online course activities, it's important to make sure the movements are safe and are done in a safe environment.

There is a balance between providing your learners with an enriched experience, and protecting yourself from legal liability. For example, if your course includes instructions to take a nature hike, collect samples, and write a report about the experience, what could go wrong, right? Well . . . a student could trip on the trail and get hurt, or get lost, or get stung by a bee and have an allergic reaction.

Would you as the course creator be liable for having sent them on the nature hike to begin with? I don't know, because, I am not an attorney, nor do I play one on TV. I can't give legal advice. I'm just raising the issue as something to think about.

When schools that have physical locations in the real world take students on field trips, they have liability insurance and field trip permission release forms and other protections in place to address issues of this nature.

I've tried doing online searches about this subject and come up with nothing. And that is not like me, because doing online research is something I'm really good at. So I'm guessing this is a relatively new area of inquiry and we are on the cutting edge right here in even thinking about it. The only thing I can suggest is that you do your own research, exercise your own due diligence, and consult with a professional such as an attorney and/or a business liability insurance expert, to see what answers you can come up with for yourself.

And then as you design your course, keep the balance in mind between providing enriching digital and real-world excursions for your students, while protecting yourself from liability for things that might potentially happen out there in the real world.

Be Mindful about the Types of Devices Your Learners May Use

For an online course, individual differences apply not just to the learner's learning style, but to the way the learner accesses your course. Some of your students will be on desktop or laptop computers, others on tablets, and many may be on smartphones these days. It's important that your course materials work with and fit onto the screen on all these devices.

Make sure your course platform uses responsive design (that is, design that responds to different screen sizes by adjusting to fit that screen).

Another type of individual difference specific to online learning has to do with how sophisticated your learners' equipment is. If you design your course with lots of fancy tech bells and whistles that look great on high-resolution screens and require fast download capabilities for streaming, your lesson may not work for someone accessing your course on an old computer or with a slow internet connection.

In addition to keeping cognitive load low for your human learners, it's important to keep the technology load low for the equipment they are using.

Let's Review

We've talked about various kinds of individual differences to keep in mind as you design your course. These differences include different learning modalities (visual, auditory, tactile, and kinesthetic), different screen sizes, and different levels of technology access.

Putting this all together, let's compare the learning experience of two theoretical learners.

- The first is a visual learner accessing a course on a high-resolution monitor from a desktop computer with excellent bandwidth for streaming video.
- The second is an auditory learner accessing the same course on a smartphone with only intermittent Wi-Fi access.

How would the learning experience differ for these two learners? What could you do as a course creator to help optimize the learning experience for both of them? It will take some forethought and advance planning to ensure that you design your course in ways that enable both learners to enjoy and benefit from the materials equally.

One way to support both learners would be to save any videos in your course as audio-only MP3 files and make those available for download for offline listening. That would help improve the learning experience of the second student.

Another consideration is printer capabilities and access. One student may have easy access to a high-speed color printer with plenty of ink, making it easy to download and print out course materials. But another student might have no printer access at all.

As you can see, all of these students will experience your online course differently.

How can you, as their instructor, account for these individual differences in learning preference and technology access? How can you do online what good teachers do in classrooms, which is to be aware of individual learning differences and ensure that each student's individual needs are met?

In your online classroom, you can achieve this teaching goal by providing your lesson material in multiple formats to allow each student to access it in the way that works best for them. You can also build variety, excitement, and universal appeal into your lessons by including activities that speak to the learner as a whole person who interacts with the world in multiple ways that extend beyond just the visual and auditory pathways.

Different Ways of Processing Information: Multiple Intelligences

Howard Gardner's theory of multiple intelligences explores the many different ways that people learn. The multiple intelligences are: [10]

- Linguistic intelligence ("word smart").
- Logical-mathematical intelligence ("number/reasoning smart").
- Spatial intelligence ("picture smart").
- Bodily kinesthetic intelligence ("body smart").
- Musical intelligence ("music smart").
- Interpersonal intelligence ("people smart").
- Intrapersonal intelligence ("self-smart").
- Naturalist intelligence ("nature smart").

While the individual learning styles (visual, auditory, tactile, and kinesthetic) focus on sensory modalities for accessing information, the multiple intelligences focus on areas of interest and ways of processing information once we have taken it in.

The frameworks describing learning styles and multiple intelligences overlap in some ways, though they are not identical. For example, someone who prefers to learn visually could have high linguistic intelligence and love to read words in books or on the screen.

But a different visual learner could dislike reading words and instead learn best by looking at pictures (spatial intelligence) or by reading music on a page (musical intelligence).

A third visual learner could learn best by walking through a forest looking at trees (naturalist intelligence).

It's understandable that someone with an auditory learning style might enjoy listening to music because they might have high musical intelligence. But an auditory learner could also be tone deaf when it comes to music and prefer listening to people speak, extracting the nuances of what someone really means by using interpersonal intelligence.

Once we combine the four learning styles with the eight multiple intelligences, there is tremendous individual variation in how people learn. Not only that, but most of us rely on more than one intelligence when we're interacting with the world. For example, the visual learner naturalist walking through the woods is also using bodily kinesthetic intelligence.

The auditory learner using interpersonal intelligence to intuit what people really mean when they speak could be using logical-mathematical intelligence to apply an algorithm that analyzes speech patterns, or bodily kinesthetic intelligence to detect variations in body language.

Considering the tremendous variety in ways of learning about the world, it seems like it would be a waste of our collective brainpower to design instruction that only meets the needs of visual and auditory learners who have high linguistic or mathematical intelligence. This narrow focus has long been a problem in classroom-based instruction, where those students who learn well by sitting quietly in a chair reading a book are rewarded as "good students," while those who can't sit still and want to get up and tinker with physical objects, or who learn through movement or by interacting with nature, are treated as troublemakers who are disrupting the class.

The advent of online learning gives us a chance to correct this societal imbalance, but we can only fix the problem if we are first aware of it. Otherwise it's too easy to get lulled into a false sense of security, thinking we have created meaningful learning that meets all learners' needs, when in fact, we are losing many of our potential learners into boredom, inattention, poor lesson retention, or other activities altogether. And if we don't have good feedback mechanisms built into our e-learning site, we won't even know that we've lost them.

The most important thing we can do, of course, is to design instruction right from the start in ways that ensure we don't lose our learners.

While the affordances and constraints of the online learning space lend themselves most easily to visual and auditory learning methods that address linguistic and mathematical intelligence, there is a lot we can do to address other learning styles and other intelligences, if we are willing to dig deeper, be creative, and "think beyond the screen."

If we restrict our way of thinking about online course design to what is possible on a screen, we restrict ourselves to designing instruction in limited ways. These limits are linked to the affordances and constraints of the online learning space. In terms of affordances, the online learning space allows us to use words, pictures, and mathematical equations, to play audio files including music, and to create or use forums in which learners can interact with each other.

Our pictures and words and audio files can include subjects dealing with movement activities and nature, too. So, on at least a superficial level, we can design instruction that addresses the learning needs of every type of intelligence. By further integrating our use of technology with learning that occurs in the outer world, we can go beyond the limits of the screen to address multiple intelligences in much deeper and more organic ways.

An article in *The American Biology Teacher* describes the way a group of biology teachers used QR codes to create a site-specific field guide for their students to use on a biology field trip.[11] The students were directed to find specific items in the natural environment, learn about the items using QR code-linked information sheets the teachers had created in advance, and then share what they learned with other members of the class using a social networking system set up by the teachers for the students' smartphones. If you're unfamiliar with QR codes, they are square blocks of computer code that a handheld scanner or smartphone can "read." When learners have the right app on their smartphones, they can scan a code their instructor gives them, and this will take them to a web page with content on it.

This brilliantly designed lesson used digital technology in several innovative ways. Instead of trying to bring nature into the online environment, the teachers used smartphones (and a lot of preplanning) to bring technology into the natural environment.

This is a very creative way to foster naturalist intelligence digitally. But the brilliance of these biology teachers' lesson plan did not stop there. The teachers had the students reinforce what they had learned by sharing photos, videos, and written messages with other members of the class. In this way they were using the ability of smartphone technology to help people connect across a distance to create a social experience right in the field. The social and emotional aspects of sharing the excitement of their finds made use of interpersonal intelligence to reinforce the naturalist learning.

The students were moving through physical space to locate the items in the field guide, which brings in kinesthetic intelligence (movement) as well as spatial intelligence needed to locate each item. The spatial intelligence was reinforced by information gained from other students over the social network, integrating naturalist, kinesthetic, and spatial intelligence with interpersonal intelligence through the use of e-learning technology.

The richness of this particular lesson derives from its use and integration of so many of the multiple intelligences in an organic and effective way.

How can you, as an educator designing instruction in an entirely online environment, achieve high levels of synthesis and integration between different multiple intelligences?

The specific ways that will be included in your course depend on the specific nature of your subject matter. Designing your instruction in ways that use multiple intelligences will make your online course meaningful and memorable for your students and will make you truly stand out from the crowd as a skilled online course designer.

The reason is that you will be thinking of your learner as a multifaceted person who interacts with the world, via your course, in richly nuanced ways. Your course will foster deep learning and engagement by appealing to your learner as a whole, multifaceted person.

Figure 12.1. Ideas for integrating learning styles and multiple intelligences in an online course. (Source: Learn and Get Smarter, Inc./Getty Images)

A Deeper Look at Bloom's Taxonomy

So far, we have looked at individual learning styles that describe how learners absorb information through the senses. And we have explored multiple intelligences that describe where learners focus their attention in the world.

Now it's time to consider the various ways learners process information about the world, once they have taken that information in through their senses. As we've previously discussed, Bloom's taxonomy is a system that classifies and organizes learners' ways of processing information from the most basic to the most advanced. The taxonomy organizes thinking skills into two major groups: lower- and higher-order thinking skills.

"Bloom's Digital Taxonomy" specifically applies Bloom's taxonomy to e-learning.[12]

As you'll recall, lower-order thinking skills include remembering, understanding, and applying what was learned. Many lessons, both on and offline, don't go beyond that point. But to truly engage the learner and make sure the subject matter has been permanently stored in long-term memory, it's important also to include the higher-order thinking skills: analyzing new information, evaluating it (or using it to evaluate other things), and creating something new that demonstrates learning has taken place.

The great news for you, as an online course creator, is that the online learning environment makes it very easy for learners to engage in higher-order thinking skills.

We've talked about the importance of building feedback mechanisms into your course so that you, and your students can be sure they have actually learned what your course is teaching them. When you think of *assessment,* do your eyelids get droopy? Do you start to yawn? *Assessment* may sound boring . . . but it doesn't have to be.

The online-learning space makes it very easy for you to engage your learners in developing higher-order thinking skills, as they create digital products or engage in interactive experiences that help them analyze and evaluate what they've learned and put it all together to come up with something new. These creative products and activities can provide feedback and serve as assessments to let you, and most importantly, your students themselves, know that they have learned what they wanted to learn, and are able to use and apply what they've learned in practical ways in their own lives.

You can and should build creative, engaging activities that serve an assessment function into your course and lesson design. Activities that require higher-order thinking skills tend to have more germane cognitive load (which is generally a good thing) than activities that only rely on lower-order thinking skills. In other words, it's more interactive and engaging to create something new based on what you've learned, than to simply parrot back facts.

It's important to be sure your students have first mastered the basics before you ask them to create something new. If you're asking your students to create something new based on what they've learned, first be sure they have learned the basics using lower-order thinking skills. Once they've done that, they will have the pre-requisite prior knowledge they need to engage effectively in more challenging creative activities.

....

THIRTEEN

MAKE SURE YOUR COURSE IS WORKING FOR ALL YOUR LEARNERS

Transformative teaching in an online context addresses your learner both as a whole person and as a unique individual. Your course will reach more students in meaningful ways if you offer multiple ways for people to access your course material, if you focus on providing them with a variety of avenues for exploring and interacting with the world, and if you help them use both lower-order and higher-order thinking skills.

It's important to do all this while remaining tightly focused on your learning objectives and managing cognitive load. That way, you will hold learners' attention without overwhelming the limits of their short-term memory.

What does this mean, technically? It means that your goal as a course designer is to help people build new schemas to store information in long-term memory, where they will have it forever, because they will have *really* learned it.

All of that is a tall enough order to begin with. Now, can you make your course materials work for students who can't see, can't hear, experience movement limitations, or face another learning challenge?

You can (because you are Super Teacher!) and we are going to discuss how you can (and why you should), in this chapter.

Making Your Materials Accessible

As online course creators, we work very hard to get people into our classrooms. The last thing we would ever want to do is keep anybody out. And once our students are in, we want to be sure they have access to our course materials, whether those are in the form of videos, audio files, PDFs, Word documents, PowerPoint or other slide presentations, and more.

The whole point of working so hard to create an online course is to invite students to take it, so they can learn from the course materials. But if we are not aware of what it takes for all our learners to access our courses and materials, we might inadvertently be keeping some of our students, or potential students, out.

The internet is a highly visual medium. We've touched on the need to compensate for this in designing instruction that appeals to nonvisual methods of taking in information, because not everyone is a visual learner. But what about those who can't see the screen at all?

The U.S. Census and other data suggest that in the years ahead, as many as one out of five Americans may face some level and type of visual impairment.[1]

There are many types of visual impairment that can affect learners' ability to access and learn from your course. Learners with complete vision loss can use screen-reading software to have your course materials read to them. Therefore, your course documents need to be set up and formatted properly so that screen-reading software can read them in ways that allow visually impaired students to benefit.

We'll talk about how to set up Word docs, PDFs, and PowerPoints to be accessible for screen readers in a minute, but first let's finish getting the big picture on what making your course accessible for learners with low or no vision, means.

The most obvious thing to think about is pictures. A picture may be worth a thousand words, but if the learner can't see the picture, it's worth exactly zero words.

The way to fix this is to use words to describe each picture in your course, so that screen readers can read that description to your student, allowing visually impaired learners to use their minds, rather than their eyes, to visualize the image.

Technically, this is done through the use of something called an *alt tag* (short for "alternative text tag"). You insert a short text snippet attached to each image, to help screen readers read it.[2]

Why am I mentioning this now? I mean, you haven't even started creating your course, right? You have no images in it yet.

Exactly. This is the perfect time to become aware of the importance of making those images "viewable" by all your students (in some situations, it's the law).

Any time you place an image in your course, your website's media library, a Word doc, or a PowerPoint or other slide presentation, make it a habit to include a short, descriptive alt tag at the same time. (This only applies to images that contain content or serve a function. Purely decorative images do not receive alt tags). Do not leave it for later—although if you do miss any images or forget to add alt tags, there is accessibility-checking software that will show you where you need to add them in. It can be done later if need be. But it's a good habit to get into to include an alt tag with every image (except those that are purely decorative), every time.

An excellent article from WebAIM explaining best practices for using alt tags can be found here: https://webaim.org/techniques/alttext.

Another thing to consider is the use of color. Learners with low vision may have trouble seeing text against a background that lacks sufficient color contrast. The highest contrast is black text on a white background. If you want to be extra sure that your learners can read the text, it's a best practice to use black text on a white background for everything.

A lot of websites these days seem to use a default medium gray color for text. I know that I personally find this very hard to read, and I do not have a vision problem. If your website defaults to a light or medium gray color for paragraph text, consider going into your appearance panel and changing the paragraph text color to black to increase the readability.

Learners with color blindness will not be able to use color cues that are built into a lesson. I discovered this the hard way in designing my master's project. At an early stage of lesson design, I asked learners to use red, green and blue to highlight different types of words. Once I started looking at accessibility issues and realized that these color cues would not work for color blind learners, I changed the instructions for the activity. Instead of using colors to highlight the words, I asked them to circle the verbs, underline the nouns, and put a triangle around the adjectives.

Of course, even the new assignment would not work for learners with no sight at all. For them, it would make more sense to ask them to create an audio recording in which they state which words are verbs, which are adjectives, and which are nouns.

A wonderful tool for checking the accessibility of any URL is the Wave Web Accessibility Evaluation Tool from WebAIM.org (see "Resources").

When learners with normal vision access a web page, they scan it to get the big picture, then home in on the parts that interest them. The first thing a reader looks at is the big page headline, to find out what this whole page is about. If that's of interest, they then skim or scan down the page to see what specific topics are covered.

When a topic of interest is found, the reader will take the time to read the small print paragraph text that goes with that headline. If the headline indicates it's not a topic the reader cares about, he or she will skip to the next headline.

Screen readers work the same way. They scan the page for the big headline, the smaller headlines (in order of importance), and then the paragraph text. But since screen readers are machines and not people and don't have eyes, they have to rely on the way a document is structured in order to do this. Screen readers use html tags to understand the document structure.[3]

While a human with normal vision can just look at the page and see which text is the biggest, which is next in size, and so on (or which is bold or emphasized in some other way), a screen reader relies on html tags to do this. The main headline needs an h1 tag to indicate it is the main headline (headline 1) on the page (there can only be one h1 tag on each page).

The next most important headings get h2 tags, then comes h3, and so on.

The paragraph text that goes with each heading gets labeled with paragraph tags (p). If you know how to write html code and are coding your site yourself, then you already know all this. But most online course creators are not writing code from scratch.

And how does this apply to documents such as Microsoft Word files or PDFs?

Microsoft Word includes a panel on the tool bar called Styles, which allows you to format your text and label it (heading 1, heading 2, and so forth). When creating a document that is going to be used in your course, it's important to use these styles to indicate which text is h1, which is h2, which is h3, which is paragraph text, and so on.[4]

Remember to add alt tags to any images, charts, or tables you include in your document.[5] You can take a course to learn how to make your online course documents accessible. WebAIM offers one I recommend (see "Resources").[6]

When you go to save your document, the best practice is always to check it to see if there are any accessibility issues you need to address. Windows 10 and Microsoft Office 365 have built-in tools to make this process much easier and more intuitive than it used to be.[7]

See "Resources" for tools that can help you check the accessibility of your documents and sites.

Once your document is accessible, you may want to turn it into a PDF for use in your course. In the process of turning your file into a PDF, take the extra steps needed to make the PDF accessible as well.[8]

If you are using a different version of software—such as Pages for a Mac computer—to create your documents, do an online search for the steps needed to use it to create an accessible PDF. Updated versions of Adobe Acrobat have tools that walk you through creating your PDF in an accessible manner. Some versions of PDF-creation software have accessibility checking built right in, so all you have to do is run that, and then fix any issues that the software reports. Many online checking tools are free. You can find a detailed list of accessibility checking tools from the W3C® Web Accessibility Initiative and other sources (see "Resources").

One solution to creating accessible versions of web-based materials is to create a text-only version. However, text-only versions, while sometimes necessary, can also create more problems than they solve.[9] Visual impairment is not the only kind of disability learners may have, and text-only formatting does not address everyone's needs. Some experts seem to feel that text-only versions do more harm than good, and that the proper procedure is to make multimedia materials accessible to begin with, natively, so that users with various disabilities can access the same course materials as everyone else.

Accessibility Has Complex Legal and Ethical Ramifications

Accessibility is a complex topic with ethical and legal ramifications. While I have taken several courses on web accessibility, I am not an expert on the subject. The information contained in this book is not a comprehensive guide to web accessibility and is not to be relied on as such. It is up to each course creator to thoroughly research and explore this subject on their own.

The goal of this chapter is to make you, as an online course creator, aware of the need to make course materials accessible so that all your students can learn from them. Think of this additional challenge as a routine part of your course and lesson development and do everything you can to develop good habits and best practices right from the start.

Aside from any legal implications, it's important not to exclude people from your course simply because they face a disability of some kind. Furthermore, considering the large number of internet users who face disabilities ranging from visual impairment and dyslexia to hearing loss or movement challenges, among others, you are leaving money on the table if you don't design your course to include and welcome all potential students. A further point is that making your materials accessible, and making them available in more than one learning modality, often makes them more usable for all your learners.

Make Sure Your Course Participants Are Learning: Feedback

So, how can you be sure your online students are actually learning? That is the most important question of all! In an online course, it's important to build ways of finding out the answer, right into the design of the course itself.

In a face-to-face setting, learning occurs in two directions. The teacher provides the students with instruction, and the students provide the teacher with feedback about how the instruction is going. Some of this feedback is automatic. You don't need to give your students a survey to see if they are bored, focused, engaged, distracted, cold, tired, and so on. Any observant teacher can automatically detect these things simply by being in the same physical space as their students and paying attention.

Some of these factors don't matter in an online course. When you no longer control the learner's physical space, it's not up to you to adjust the thermostat if the room they are in is too hot or cold. You've been relieved of that responsibility. You also don't need to make sure your students have chairs, or are not hungry, or give them a restroom break. All of that is on them.

But you do need to know if they are paying attention, if they understand the material, and if they are properly absorbing it. You need to know if they are emotionally present, socially focused, and intellectually engaged.

Most of all, you need to know if they have actually learned the material in each lesson. You need to be sure they have built the new schemas that will serve as prior knowledge for the next lesson in your course before you let them move on to that next lesson.

Many online course systems have attempted to regulate this factor by using a drip feature for the release of new instruction. Personally and professionally, as both teacher and student, I am not a huge fan of the drip feature in online teaching, and I will tell you why. The drip feature puts control of the pace of instruction in the hands of the teacher, not the student. This directly violates one of the best practices for online learning in adult learners, which is to allow the learner to control the pace of instruction.[10]

It does not respect the autonomy of an adult learner to have someone else tell them when they can and cannot go on to the next lesson. It also does not do what it is supposed to do. The assumption behind dripping instruction is that the student needs a certain amount of time to complete each lesson, and therefore the next lesson should not be released before that amount of time has passed. However, some students are fast learners who are highly focused and engaged. Forcing them to wait for the next lesson only serves to dilute their focus, interest, and momentum toward completing the course.

This recently happened to me in an otherwise excellent online course I'm taking. I finished a module and was ready, willing, and able to move on to the next one. I had the time, the energy, and the space in my schedule—and for many adult learners that is a rare thing. But I couldn't go on to the next module because I had to wait an hour and a half until they released it. That was the exact hour and a half I would have had available to work on that module! I rest my case.

Some students prefer to first get an overview of the whole course, and then go back to complete the lessons in sequence. These learners need a clear picture of the whole in order to understand how all the parts fit into it.

Other students have a specific time period available in their schedules for completing a course. If the course's drip schedule doesn't allow them to complete it on their own timetable, they may not have the time to complete it later. That's exactly what happened to me in the example I shared above.

The fact that a specific amount of time has passed is no guarantee that the student has completed a lesson, or, most importantly, has learned from it. If you want to release lessons in step-by-step fashion to be sure the student has properly built in the prior knowledge they need for the next lesson, the way to do that is by making successful completion of each lesson a prerequisite for moving on to the next. It makes sense to release lessons based on a learner's successful completion of earlier lessons. It does not (except in a few specific types of situations) make sense to release lessons based on how much time has passed.

Using a time-based drip feature makes sense only in situations where time is the controlling factor. For example, if you are running a ten-day challenge, it makes sense to drip out each day's content one day at a time. Or if group participation in a learning cohort requires that everyone start a specific lesson at the same time so they can work on it together, then time-based dripping makes sense there too. But as a general practice, many adult learners will not be able to consume a course in the way that works best for them if a time-based drip feature is used.

Some course-management systems make it easy to release new lessons based on assessment of earlier ones, others don't. But you as the instructor can set up your course to do that, if you want.

My argument would be not to force your student to pass the assessment before going on to later lessons. Maybe they already know they know the material and want to jump in at the point where things start to get interesting for them. As teachers of adult learners who are taking a course of their own free will, we are not policemen, we are partners in their learning journey. Our job is to structure that learning journey effectively, and then support them as they navigate it according to their own interests, autonomy, timetable, and skills.

That said, I've had students request that each lesson be made a prerequisite for the next. The advantage of allowing learners to control the pace of instruction may be outweighed by the added cognitive load some learners experience when they see all the lessons spread out before them at once. In that case, my suggestion is to make successfully completing one lesson, a prerequisite for releasing the next, but *not* to resort to a time-based drip method.

Seek direct feedback from your students as to what does and doesn't work well for them. Part of getting feedback about how your learners are experiencing your course, involves observing what happens when they actually interact with the lessons. When it comes to respecting the choices and autonomy of adult learners, the best way to get feedback about how well your instruction and delivery systems are meeting their needs is to ask them for it.

Just as too much of the teaching focus online today is on making money, too much of the feedback request focus is on getting testimonials. There is nothing wrong with either making money or getting testimonials, but neither should be the main reason for getting feedback. The main reason for teaching is to help your students learn, and the appropriate main reason for getting feedback is to make sure that they are in fact learning.

It's important to embed multiple types of feedback into your course. You are going to need continual ongoing feedback about whether your students can access and navigate the online course materials, whether they can understand them, and whether they have learned what you are teaching in the lesson.

The issue of ensuring your learners can get into and use your online learning portal is technology based. Although you are not responsible for the room temperature and the number of desks and chairs, you are responsible for making sure your students can get into the online classroom and use all of its features. There should be some way for students to let you (or someone else who can help them) know at all times whether the technology that supports your course is working.

Some course platforms build those types of tech support issues into the features the platform provides. If your chosen platform doesn't do that, or if you are hosting the course yourself on your own website, it's important to have some way for your students to let you know if they can't log in or need tech help of any kind.

It's not enough simply to ask for feedback; it's also important to acknowledge that it's been received. The next important thing to do is either implement the suggestions made or explain why a specific suggestion or request cannot be accommodated at this time.

Some course creators handle this type of ongoing feedback via a private Facebook or other social media group for their class. You could also build it into the course platform or handle it by email. It doesn't matter so much *how* you ask for feedback, as *that* you ask for it, and that you *use it* to make your course continually more responsive to students' needs.

PART FOUR

TEST AND REFINE TO MAKE
YOUR COURSE SHINE

FOURTEEN

....

HOW TO ADAPT FACE-TO-FACE LEARNING TO ONLINE (AND HOW NOT TO)

When I work with experts who have existing, successful, classroom-based courses or workshops they want to put online, the first thing they tell me is that they have to go through many hours of video (that they've taken of their live in-person classes) in order to select footage to create an online course. It's only normal to think that the way to adapt face-to-face learning to online is to simply film or otherwise digitize the in-person experience and upload the content to a website where learners can access it.

That approach, however, does not work to create an effective and engaging online course. It is a slow, tedious, and time-consuming process that leads to poor results.

How do I know this? I know because I was one of those experts myself, and I am going to share my experiences and discoveries with you as a case study for what works and what does not. My experiences and discoveries involved running into many failure points at which it became clear that what I was doing would not work.

If you're in a hurry to create your online course and don't want to focus on how I developed the Course Design Formula®, or the philosophy behind it, you can skip this chapter for now. But I hope you won't, because understanding the reasons for following the steps in this book is an important part of making those steps work. If you do skip this chapter for now, I hope you'll come back to it later. The information in this chapter may mean even more to you once you've grappled with getting your own course online. On the other hand, it will be a lot easier for you to *get* your course online if you learn upfront from what I discovered (the hard way) doesn't work.

Learning from What Doesn't Work

Let's go on a journey back in time to learn how the Course Design Formula® came to be.

A long, long time ago, I was creating an online course as the final project for my master's degree in instructional technology. I was creating it, but like many of the experts I've worked with since, I didn't realize that I needed to *design* it first. I thought I could just take what I was already doing in classroom settings, transfer it to digital media, and *voila,* I would have an online course.

Let me tell you about some of the things I discovered do not work, so you won't have to discover them yourself (you're welcome).

I had wanted the topic of my course to be "How to Teach Anything to Anyone Online," but my project advisor said I had to pick a much narrower topic. (Picking the topic was one of the most difficult parts of the whole project, and I find that it is also difficult for many of my students and clients to narrow down exactly what they want their course topic to be.) My first plan was to recreate my existing classroom-based education program in an online format.

I worked for public agencies where I was the education coordinator in charge of designing, developing, and delivering education programs about water and energy conservation for local schools. I had spent fifteen years designing instruction to be delivered (by me) in person. It was the ideal situation for a learning designer. Not only did I get to design and develop the learning programs and materials myself, I also got to deliver the programs in classrooms, where I received constant and ongoing feedback straight from the "end users" (students). Delivering presentations live in classrooms, laboratories, and field facilities multiple times a week for fifteen years provided the ideal opportunity to create instruction that was dynamic, effective, and perfectly tailored to its target audience.

I decided it was time to put that perfectly tailored in-person instruction online, because I wanted to be able to reach more people with a water and energy conservation message. I wanted people to be able to learn what I was teaching, any time they wanted, on demand.

Please note that I had *already* followed an instructional design process in creating my classroom-based presentations. The fascinating (though at the time, extremely frustrating) thing though, was that those beautifully designed and thoroughly tested classroom-based lessons did not work the same way online. It took me several years and a master's degree to figure out why. (One of the main reasons has to do with what happens to your course's previously well-balanced cognitive load when you move your material online.)

What I discovered, and want to share with you in this chapter, is that knowing how to present your content in person can actually make it harder, not easier, to figure out how to present the same material online.

The reason for that is that while you have prior knowledge about how to present your material effectively, it's the *wrong* prior knowledge for how to present it effectively online. The online teaching situation imposes different affordances and constraints on the way you present the material, and it changes the way cognitive load works. Even if you've had cognitive load perfectly balanced in your classroom presentation, putting your course online is going to upset the apple cart.

What I advise experts and entrepreneurs to do is to take all of their apples (course content) *out* of the apple cart (course structure) and put that content aside until they've got the online version of the course set up using the Course Design Formula®. Once you've got the course structured efficiently for online teaching, it will be quick and easy to insert your content where it will work best for the online version. But if you remain attached to the way you are presenting your content face-to-face, you will have a harder time restructuring it for effective online teaching.

It's important to me to share the stories in this chapter with you, because I hear many experts and entrepreneurs say that they don't need to apply an instructional design process to their content, because they're already teaching it in person. That was what I thought, too. Everything you're about to read, I learned from doing what I hear others say they are going to do. I discovered the following principles as a result of trying things that didn't work.

Failure Point 1: You Can't Just Digitize Classroom-based Instruction and Get an Effective Online Course

My first failure happened before I even got into my master's project, and was one of the main reasons I decided to go back to school to get a master's degree in instructional technology.

The first thing I tried, which is the first thing most people try, was to video one of my live classroom presentations. The classroom presentation was dynamic and engaging and got great results when presented live. The digital version, however, would have scared small children (which was not good, since small children were my actual target audience for the presentation).

Why was it scary? In person, I am warm and engaging. I can respond to questions on the fly and I have fun materials and activities to hand out. (Sometimes I even have chocolate!) On film, however, I did not come across the same way. The film version was long, boring, unengaging, and flat.

Watching that shudder-inducing film, I had an aha moment about why movie stars have to be so physically attractive. In a movie, the visual sense is the only way to interact with someone. You don't have the immediacy of direct personal contact, ongoing feedback, inter-personal exchange (and sometimes, chocolate). So, the visual sense has to be punched up to a much higher level to achieve the same intensity and interactivity you get from the multisensory experience that live teaching provides.

I realized that in order for a filmed presentation to be fun and engaging, you need good lighting (which the classroom didn't have). You need a short, targeted script created specifically for video (which my classroom-based presentation didn't have). And you need the acting skill and physical beauty of a movie star (which I personally didn't have).

Remember, what we are talking about relates to the topic of affordances and constraints. Affordances are things that a specific situation, context, or medium allows you to do easily and well, while constraints are things that that situation, context, or medium makes it difficult or impossible to do.[1]

The live classroom situation afforded me the ability to interact directly with the class in a warm and personal way, whereas my video did not. The video simply was not able to capture and replicate the immediacy of the original experience for an audience watching online.

That was my first aha moment, when I realized there was more to creating online instruction than simply digitizing existing material that works well in the physical world.

The Importance of Having the *Right* Prior Knowledge

If you already know Italian and now you want to learn Spanish, your prior knowledge of Italian will make learning Spanish easier. Because both are romance languages derived from Latin and share similar grammar, vocabulary, and rules, you will be able to adapt the schemas you've already built for learning Italian to help you learn Spanish. Relevant prior knowledge is helpful. However, sometimes our prior knowledge can get in the way of new learning, rather than being helpful.

I discovered this with respect to language learning when I had the opportunity to visit Istanbul, Turkey, on vacation. I love languages and learn them easily, and I already know English (of course), several romance languages, and languages from the Semitic language family, which includes Hebrew and Arabic. So, I had lots of language schemas already established in my brain's permanent storage area.

However, none of the language rules I already knew were helpful in figuring out road signs or billboards in Istanbul. Although I had a lot of prior knowledge for learning languages, it was the wrong prior knowledge for learning Turkish. This problem is so common in language learning that there is an actual term for it, *language interference.*[2]

I was so intrigued by this problem that I eventually used it as the basis for the course I designed for my master's project. Since the rules for learning many other languages wouldn't help for learning Turkish, what rules would help? What was the useful prior knowledge that an English, French, or Arabic speaker would need in order to make learning Turkish easier?

My goal for the master's project was not to teach Turkish. (That would have been a poor topic choice, considering I don't speak Turkish myself.) Rather, my goal was *first* to discover a specific set of rules—the rules that work for learning Turkish—and *then* to figure out how to teach those rules online.

Failure Point 2: Be Sure an Online Course Is the Solution to the Problem You're Trying to Solve

You may notice that the topic I ended up using for my project was far removed from the presentations about water and energy I had originally planned to create. That actually turned out to be a good thing. I had so much prior knowledge about water and energy that I was very attached to my classroom-based presentations. It was hard for me to let go of what I knew worked well in the classroom long enough to discover what might work better for teaching the same material online. My prior knowledge about how to teach my material was the wrong prior knowledge. Many of my clients and students also find it hard to let go of what they know works in a classroom setting, in order to create something that will work online. (The Course Design Formula® is designed to make it easy for you to let go of this unhelpful prior knowledge so you can get your course online, fast.)

Before deciding to create an education program or course of any kind (online or offline), it is important first to determine that instruction is the right solution for the problem you are trying to solve.3 For example, let's say that a workplace is having a problem with employees smoking too much in the parking lot during breaks. Before deciding to implement an education program about the dangers of smoking, it would be a good idea to find out why they are smoking so much. If it turns out the increased smoking is due to stress caused by new company policies, then the solution to the smoking problem would be better addressed by revising those policies than by teaching people that smoking is bad for you (which they probably already know).

If instruction *is* the answer, consider the next question: Is *online* instruction the answer?

One thing I discovered in the process of choosing the topic for my project was that for my original topic choice, the answer was no.

My existing classroom-based water and energy conservation program was working beautifully for my agency's needs. Although I could see value in adding an online component (I was hoping to reach more students in less time), creating an entirely online version would have worked against one of my agency's main goals for the conservation program, which was to have a representative of our agency reach out in person to teachers and students in local schools. So that, among other reasons, is why I abandoned the idea of taking my classroom-based program online. I decided instead to do my masters project on a totally unrelated topic: teaching a basic grammar rule that would help speakers of other languages understand a fundamental aspect of Turkish.

As I've said, I am not an expert on Turkish. Other than some basic greetings, I don't even speak it! It was my lack of expertise that made me curious to understand the rules that make this language work. Not being an expert in the subject matter turned out to be a very helpful thing, because I did not experience the *expert blind spot* many experts struggle with when figuring out how to present their subject matter.[4] Having expertise can make it hard for teachers to be aware of what they know that their learners don't know.

In the case of my master's project, I didn't know anything about Turkish, so there was no expert blind spot problem at all. And since I was no longer trying to take my existing classroom based program online, I no longer had to worry about having the "wrong" prior knowledge—knowledge about what made my program work in the classroom environment. Being attached to your prior knowledge about what makes the classroom version of your course work can be a major hindrance in creating an online version of that same course.

How I Discovered and Developed the Course Design Formula®

Now that I had a topic for my master's project course, I set out to create it.

For my first prototype, I tried creating a course that had logical sections, of the type you would use if you were giving a lecture or presentation. I wanted to make the course engaging and interesting, so my first thought was, *Let's include lots of beautiful pictures of Turkey.* I had taken these pictures myself and thought they would help learners engage with my course by providing local color and contrast.

Failure Point 3: Not Understanding What's Fundamental to Making an Online Course Effective

People loved the pictures I chose for my prototype. But they did not learn anything from them about the rules of Turkish grammar, because the pictures had no relevance to the actual topic of the course. This was an important aha moment. Everything in a course must be directly relevant to the course's learning goal. If your course teaches the rules of Turkish grammar, then scenic pictures of the Bosphorus Strait are irrelevant. This correlates with multimedia best practices described by Ruth Clark and Richard Mayer, emphasizing that all media included in a course must serve an educational, rather than a purely decorative purpose.[5]

Another mistake I made was to start creating my course based on media decisions, rather than instructional design decisions. In Chapter 9 we discussed why media selection needs to be one of the last steps you take in creating your course, not one of the first. I discovered that by doing it wrong and realizing it didn't work. If you start creating media before completely designing the learning journey you want learners to take through your content, you may end up creating learning materials you will have to scrap later. That's what happened to me—more than once.

Failure Point 4: Outlining Your Course the Same Way You Would Outline a Lecture or Presentation

If you're an expert on a topic, you may have been invited to give a lecture or presentation summarizing what you know. It's natural to prepare for this type of talk by writing an outline. Most audience members who attend such presentations pick up a few useful pointers or tips. They gain an overview of the expert's research and professional experience. But listening to an hour-long presentation won't enable the audience members to *do* all the things that the speaker can do. And that's OK, because no one expects anything different from an hour-long lecture.

The problem is that many experts and entrepreneurs try to outline an online course the same way they would outline an hour-long lecture. They provide a summary or overview of their expertise from their own point of view. But this type of outline doesn't work to teach others how to do what you do. It's fine for telling people *about* what you do, but not for helping them learn to actually *do it* for themselves.

In order to help others learn the skills you have mastered, you have to outline your course from the learner's perspective, rather than from your own.

As an expert, it's nearly impossible to see your subject matter from the learner's perspective, because you can't "unknow" what you know. But you can tap into a different kind of expertise to help you build a course: expertise relating to how people best learn the specific type of material your course teaches. (How they will learn your material best depends on whether you are teaching verbal information, attitudes, motor skills, and so on.)

For creating an online course, you need a teaching outline that produces a series of events that promote learning.

I was lucky in *not* being an expert on Turkish for my master's degree. Because I was not an expert on the topic, I had to find another way to create my course outline. I was interested in Gagné's research on how people learn different types of material, and I knew that my course was going to teach the type of material Gagné calls intellectual skills, so I looked at how his research suggests people learn that type of material, best.

The topic of Turkish vowel harmony (a fundamental aspect of Turkish grammar) was a lucky choice, because learning how to apply Turkish vowel harmony turns out to be an excellent example of an intellectual skill. Intellectual skills require learners to apply a set of rules:

if this condition applies, *then* do that.[6] What I discovered, by trial and error, while designing my course, was that following Gagné's guidelines for teaching an intellectual skill made my course design come together in a clear and effective way. The other things I tried all led to frustrating and time-consuming failure points, but following Gagné's guidelines worked fast and well.[7]

After completing my master's project, I expanded my exploration to look at what Gagné's research tells us about how people learn other types of information. Then I created a framework for setting up online course structures in each of the five domains of learning Gagné defined—and which you've been reading about in this book.

In the years that followed, I tested the framework with experts who were creating online courses in a wide variety of fields. The course outline structures suggested by Gagné's research worked elegantly to quickly create effective course designs for any course on any topic. And that is how I created the Course Design Formula®.

The Course Design Formula® will help you quickly and easily develop a course outline that produces transformative learning for any type of subject matter.

The reason it works is that it helps you create your course outline from the *learner's* point of view.

But wait . . . I wasn't done failing yet (and discovering amazing, powerful instructional design truths that can help you, as a result).

Failure Point 5: Creating Engaging Activities That Do Not Fit the Course Learning Goal

If you are an experienced teacher in classroom, field, and workshop settings, you know how to think on your feet and create effective learning experiences by instinct. At this point in your career, you have reached the point of *unconscious competence*. That means that you perform well instinctively, without having to think about it.[8]

Many experts who want to create an online course are at the stage of unconscious competence in their areas of expertise.

My analogy for unconscious competence is that it's like being an old-world grandma who's been cooking the ancestral soup in her well-stocked home kitchen for so long that she doesn't have to think about it. She doesn't use a recipe. She acts on instinct—and her instincts are so well honed, her ingredients so well-seasoned, so thoroughly tested and tried, that her soup comes out delicious every time, and everyone loves it.

But what happens to our old-world grandma (and her soup!) if we take her out of her traditional kitchen stocked with familiar herbs and spices, and plunk her down in a modern industrial test kitchen designed for high-production value, global reach, and speed? The ingredients found in the industrial test kitchen are not the same as the ones our expert grandma is used to cooking with at home. The cooking methods are different. The affordances (things you can do easily in this context) and the constraints (things you can do poorly or not at all) have changed. And because Grandma is used to acting on instinct and doesn't have a deeper understanding of the abstract principles behind the specifics that made her soup come out great in her old environment, she's stuck now trying to figure out how to make an equally delicious and satisfying soup under the new conditions found in the industrial test kitchen.

That's what it was like for me when I first left my familiar workspace of the face-to-face teaching environment for the industrial test kitchen of teaching online. I did what any old-world grandma would do: I tried mixing up a batch of the familiar soup, with the spices and flavorings I knew worked well when teaching in person.

For example, I wanted the learning activities in my online course to be fun and engaging, so I decided to create a linguistic scavenger hunt. It wasn't until I had put a lot of work into creating this activity that I realized my learners lacked the prior knowledge of Turkish needed to make it work. Sure, the internet afforded people the opportunity to visit live websites in Turkish, but the activity was too hard for my target audience. Being able to navigate a website in Turkish was not directly relevant to the learning goal, which was to understand how a specific grammar feature worked.

Are you starting to notice a pattern? I did. I started to notice that the various failure points were often caused by including things in the course that did not lead *directly* to the course's learning goal.

Online instruction has to be designed a lot more tightly than classroom-based instruction, because the teacher is not there in person to guide learners and see how they are doing. A lot of the mental processing space needed to learn new things in an online course gets used up by interpreting instructions, navigating the interface, and operating more independently than one does in a face-to-face learning environment.[9]

The various failure points I encountered in my rapid prototyping process made it clear that an online course must have a very clearly defined learning goal—and that everything included in the course must lead directly *to* that goal. Anything else you include will be extraneous, and will only serve to waste your time, and your students'.

Summary of Time-Saving Lessons Learned

From a left-brained perspective, I developed the Course Design Formula® by integrating my professional observations and experiences relating to teaching and learning, with the research findings of educational theorists such as Robert M. Gagné, Jean Piaget, Jerome Bruner, and others.

From a right-brained perspective, I had to unpack my own unconscious competence and work backward to discover the core principles that would make it fast and easy to design an effective online course, without getting lost in sidetracks, detours, quagmires, and swamps.

I discovered where the quagmires and swamps in the course design process lay by wandering into them and getting stuck in "mud," as described above. To save you from going through the same thing, here's a quick summary of what I learned:

- You can't just digitize classroom-based instruction and get an effective online course.
- Your online course must be the solution to a specific problem that people care about solving.
- Your course must have a single clear, specific, overarching learning goal.
- You must understand what's fundamental to making your course effective.
- You can't outline your course as if it were a talk for a lecture or presentation.
- Everything in your course must lead directly to the course's learning goal.

....

WHAT YOU NEED TO CREATE A TRANSFORMATIVE COURSE

If you think back on the various learning experiences you've had, where you were the student, some will stand out as very positive. The reason those learning experiences stand out is because of the teacher you had.

A Teaching Mindset

Some teachers have that special knack for making you feel truly seen and cared about as a learner. They have a deep knowledge of and love for the subject matter that makes you love it and want to know more about it too. And they have a subtle yet skillful way of infusing their knowledge of the subject matter into your brain, so that you almost learn by osmosis, without understanding how it's happening.

These are the master teachers who truly help you learn and get smarter.

The purpose of this book is to help you be that teacher in your students' lives: the one they look back on, even years later, and remember with gratitude, because you truly changed their lives and helped them achieve goals that mattered to them.

Transformative Teaching

So, what is transformative teaching, exactly?

It is teaching that nurtures the student by providing an understanding, safe space in which to grow. It is teaching so well and skillfully designed that the student can't help moving along the path from point A to point B, that represents the next steps needed to master the subject matter.

Transformative teaching requires that you demonstrate skill in three dimensions, which are:

- Subject matter knowledge.
- Teaching skill (which online means, instructional design skill).
- Understanding learners' needs.

Subject matter knowledge is outside the scope of this book. Whatever it is that you are planning to teach, you will have already learned it from other sources before deciding to design an online course.

Teaching skill is something you may have already developed in other contexts, before deciding to teach online. You may already be a transformative teacher in a classroom, workshop, or presentation setting. It's also possible that you have already tried one or more times to build an online course and not loved the result. When you first started teaching online, you might have tried to do the same things you do in your real-world classes, only to discover that they don't work online. Your previous online classes may have conveyed information well enough, but felt dull, boring, lifeless, and lacking in that special connection and spark you wanted them to have.

No matter. If you apply what you've learned in this book, you'll be able to adapt and adjust your repertoire of teaching skills, to give your online courses the same student-centered focus as your face-to-face ones.

Because we don't usually directly see our students in an online class, it is harder to focus on their needs. But you can build in structures that help you "see" your students in your online class through proper use of guided practice, feedback, and assessment. Structuring your course using proper design principles helps you provide a safe and nurturing online-learning experience.

Design Your Course Tightly

In order to create a warm and nurturing learner experience conducive to transformation in an online course, the course designer paradoxically has to be very strict and hard-nosed in applying design principles that can feel a bit rigid and harsh. Warm, fuzzy design techniques (such as going with the flow and following your gut) may feel creatively satisfying to the course creator, but they do not lead to good learning outcomes for the learner in the long term.

From teaching the Course Design Formula® Master Course to my own online students, and observing their results, I have discovered that the rules I am teaching you here can't be broken if you want to achieve a good learning result. These are not rules that can be voted on and changed, like the rules of a club. These are rules of nature, like the law of gravity. These rules are based on how people learn. The internet and algorithms and artificial intelligence may be evolving at a rapid rate, but our brains aren't.

Digital media may afford us the ability to do certain things. But we should only do those things if they help human learners achieve the course learning goal. The purpose of your course is to help *humans* achieve a specific transformation. This means that your course must be designed based on how the human brain processes information.

Discovery Learning vs. Guided Instruction

There has been a debate among educators regarding the efficacy of different ways of approaching learning and teaching. One school of thought, represented by educational theorists such as Jerome Bruner and Jean Piaget, advocates allowing learners to explore and come to their own discoveries about the world, much as children do when engaging in free play.[1] The other school of thought, represented by educational theorists such Richard Mayer, Paul Kirschner, John Sweller, and Richard Clark, finds that learning must be tightly focused, structured, and controlled in order to ensure that learners learn what they need to.[2]

Which school of thought is right?

It turns out they both are, but only when placed in the right context.

Research has shown that in the online context, unguided discovery learning is not as efficient as guided, structured, step-by-step learning.[3] This is because the learner is as likely to "discover" incorrect or irrelevant information as to arrive at the desired learning goal.[4] Therefore, the guided part of guided discovery is of critical importance in ensuring a successful learning outcome in e-learning. Providing structured, step-by-step guided practice that leads directly to the learning goal is especially helpful for learners who don't have much prior knowledge relating to the subject matter.[5]

Why Online Learning Needs to Be Tightly Structured

Online learners have choices that are not your course. Many people learn what they need or want to learn from free online resources, such as publicly available YouTube videos or publicly searchable blog posts. People can gain information by finding forums dedicated to the topic they are interested in or by looking up journal articles on their own.

So, why do people sign up and pay for online courses? They do that because they are expecting the course to provide something different from what they can get on their own. On their own, they can get bits and pieces of information that answer a specific question or teach a specific skill. What they are seeking from an online course, however, goes beyond information. They are seeking *transformation*. They want to go from being a person who is at point A to a person who is at point B, a person who possesses the talents and abilities and skill sets that can only be found at point B, the course learning goal.

The extra value that learners expect from an online course is a curated, integrated, step-by-step journey put together by someone who understands the subject matter, and who also understands how people can best *learn* that specific subject matter. What people pay for when they purchase an online course is a guarantee that they are going to end up at point B.

This is not that different than what people do when they pay for a treadmill, an elliptical machine, or a gym membership. Now, if you pay for a treadmill, and the treadmill is in good working order, but you never use it . . . you can't expect to get results. That's what happened to me with my Egyptian hieroglyphics course. I don't blame the course creator for my not having learned that course material, because it was my own fault for giving up too easily. (On the other hand, if the course material had been easier to access and had provided me with more immediate tangible results, I might not have given up so easily).

But what if you pay for a gym membership and go to the gym every day, and you even pay extra to work out one-on-one with a personal trainer, and you are good on your diet and don't cheat . . . and then after three months of doing everything you paid for and were told to do, you did not get any results? (I'm getting upset just thinking about it, aren't you?). That's what happens when online courses don't take the learner all the way to point B as promised.

The reason courses don't get learners all the way to the intended transformation is that the road that gets from point A to point B, the course's instructional design roadmap, does not go all the way through. If an online course is not properly designed, then even if the learner does everything they are instructed to, they still will not get the promised result of ending up at point B. That's because the course itself has not been constructed in a way that gets the learner to point B.

The Course Design Formula® uses a backward design process to *ensure* your learners end up at point B. They have to, because you've first clearly defined point B, and then built your course backward from there.

So, one reason an online course needs to be so carefully constructed is that it needs to be a clear, direct pathway through the complex information jungle of the internet, leading directly from Point A (where your learners are starting from) to Point B (the course learning goal). If your course's path is not clear and well designed, learners can all too easily wander off that path and end up somewhere else.

Another reason to tightly design your course is that the online learning situation in and of itself imposes demands on learners' working memory, adding to cognitive load. Mayer, Moreno and Clark provide specific guidelines for how to address this phenomenon when designing your course.[6] Their suggestions include many of the things we've discussed in other contexts. (*The fact that these guidelines appear as the solutions to multiple problems in online learning tells us how important it is to follow them.*) These critical guidelines are to:

- Use pictures to provide context for related text.
- Present new information in small chunks.
- Provide explicit guidance on how to process each chunk.
- Remove anything that doesn't absolutely have to be there.

Tightly structuring your course does not mean that you can't include creative and fun learning activities in it. The true art and skill that master teachers possess is the art and skill of seamlessly structuring learning in a way that unobtrusively leads learners to discover answers or develop skills for themselves. In my experience, discovery learning can work and does work, even in the high-cognitive-load environment of online learning, if you design a learning path that tightly guides your learners to make the discoveries you want them to make, for themselves.[7] That's what the Course Design Formula® is designed to help you do.

As you already know, the Course Design Formula® guides you to put a lot of thought and planning, up front, into how you are going to build your course. The goal is to help both you and your students stay on track at every step, and ensure you design your course as the shortest and most direct route possible between your learners' starting point and the course learning goal.

This way of designing your course takes work, but the end result is a powerfully transformative learning journey that will take your learners directly where you want them to go.

SIXTEEN

....

CREATE EFFECTIVE, SKILLFUL, AND ELEGANT LEARNING

*E*legant teaching* is a term I made up to describe the way skilled teachers gracefully layer multiple teaching techniques into a single activity. One of the hallmarks of elegant teaching is that an instructor becomes adept at accomplishing more than one thing at a time.

Let's use a classroom-based example to illustrate this point. Imagine you are teaching kindergarten and want a way to get a class of five-year-olds to line up to go to lunch. An unskillful and inexperienced teacher might just look at the clock, yell at the students to stop what they're doing, tell them all to line up at once, and then spend time and energy yelling some more as the students jostle each other for position, talk loudly in line, try to dash out the door to lunch, and so on.

An experienced and skillful teacher, on the other hand, might handle lining the class up for lunch like this:

- Ring a bell when it's time for the students to start putting their work away (auditory cue, gaining attention).
- Play a jingle or song when it's time to get ready to line up.
- Have a series of circles, triangles, squares of various colors painted on the floor of the classroom at locations where she wants the line to form (visual cue).
- Look for the first student who is sitting quietly with hands folded, work put away, ready to go to lunch (social and behavioral cues).
- Say "I invite Sandra to stand on a yellow triangle" (kinesthetic learning, visual learning, social learning, spatial learning).
- When Sandra is on the yellow triangle, as a reward she gets to call on the next student who is "ready" and invite that child to stand on a specific color and shape (social reinforcement of desired behaviors, rewarding desired behaviors, visual learning, kinesthetic learning, auditory learning, spatial learning, community building).

With all that going on, there is no need for crowd-control techniques (that don't even work), yelling, or creating negative feelings in the class. The teacher is skillfully integrating the kindergarten curriculum's learning goals about colors, shapes, proper behavior, taking turns, and more with the routine activity of getting ready to go to lunch.

Doing things this way subtly but powerfully teaches desired behaviors, such as working hard, overcoming obstacles, thinking outside the box, and so forth. The more one can integrate multiple layers and facets of the teaching situation in a graceful way, the better. Those facets include the factors of logistics, management, planning, and assessment, along with the learning goals that are the heart of the teaching endeavor.

What about online learning? How can we achieve this same level of elegance when teaching adults online? Although it's simple to follow, the Course Design Formula® is based on a complex understanding of how people learn different types of material. The formula guides you to build the learning goals, types of learning, and behavior cues you want to reinforce into your course at the appropriate places, empowering you to skillfully incorporate elegance into your course design.

Remember, the rules I'm teaching you aren't rules that you can change depending on how you feel about them. These rules are like the law of gravity. Break them at your peril.

The reason you can't break these rules (if you want your students to really learn from your course) is that they are fundamental to how the human brain takes in, processes, and stores information. These rules are fundamental to how deep learning occurs.

Technology is evolving at a rapid rate, but we're not. And when designing for human learning, it's the *constraints* of *human* intelligence (not the *affordances* of *artificial* intelligence) that matter. Technology must serve the requirements of human learning if an online course is going to achieve its goal, which is to help people actually learn.

When piloting my own first course on online instructional design, every time I heard howls of pain from my students it was because I had inadvertently broken one of these rules.

Rebecca, you may be thinking, *how could you break one of these rules? You just wrote a book on them!*

Yes, I did. But it's not always obvious how the rules should be applied, or how they are going to work best in any specific course. For example, I had assumed that my course participants would be eager to jump right into designing their own courses, so I skipped over a lot of the theoretical background and had them begin at the practical part.

If you've been paying attention to how to design a course that teaches intellectual skills (how-to skills), you'll notice the big glaring error I made, right there. In an intellectual skills course that teaches a complex skill, it's important to present the big ideas first, and only then take your learners through the action steps.

I started with the action steps. (Mistake! Don't do it!) And then I had to backtrack to fill in the big ideas and clarify the important discriminations, such as the different levels of a course. I was not perfect in designing my course and I am giving you permission to be imperfect in designing yours. Doing things imperfectly at first is a natural part of learning anything new.

This process is not about starting out perfect, because that's not a realistic goal for anyone. It's about learning a way of thinking about course design that will enable you to get feedback about what's not working well for your course participants, understand *why* it's not working well, and fix it immediately.

When I started hearing howls of pain from my own course participants, the Course Design Formula® made it fast and easy for me to see where the problem was. Knowing the rules for how an intellectual skill *should* be taught, and realizing where I had *deviated* from those rules, made it easy for me to get back on track quickly. I suppose you might even consider my breaking of those rules another of my "failure points". What I learned from that failure point is that it really doesn't work to ignore these rules, period. Ever.

I see my former students doing this now with their own courses. They are able to tell whether something isn't working due to too much cognitive load, incorrect domain of learning, structural problems, or any other reason, and they are able to course correct (yes, I said that) quickly and effectively.

The instructional design process you've been learning to use in this book is repeatable and adaptable. It gives you the tools you need to create effective and engaging courses on any type of subject matter for any audience. With practice, you'll become increasingly skillful at using those tools to keep making your courses better, clearer, more engaging, and more motivating. This system puts you in control of the complex process of arranging a series of events that promote learning, which is how Gagné defined teaching.

As you continue to test your course and get feedback, you'll have a solid framework that helps you understand what's working, what's not working, and why. You'll be able to see when the events in your course are not arranged optimally, because you'll be monitoring the learning that results. And you'll have the insights and skills you need to optimize anything that needs to be optimized.

How do you monitor and optimize your course?

Beta test. Pilot. Revise.

Test, Iterate, Refine

An online course is a living thing (at least, it should be), because the learner experience is an important aspect of the course. From your first beta tester to your ultimate testimonial, what you learn about how your course is working in actual practice, matters. It matters more than anything else, because the whole point of your course is to help people learn.

That's why it's important to be open minded and professional when listening to learner feedback. Understanding the principles in this book will help you understand why you are getting specific types of feedback, and how to correct anything that is not helping your course participants learn. You are also invited to join the community of course creators I lead on Facebook, where you can ask questions and get help (see "Next Steps").

Be Open to Constant Feedback

As we've previously discussed, one of the main differences between face-to-face teaching and teaching online is that face-to-face teaching provides you with constant feedback in real time. If your students are bored or not paying attention, you'll see it in their faces. If they're trying to do something else and your course at the same time, that will be pretty obvious. If they're confused, you'll see the puzzled looks and lack of forward progress. And you can stop and ask them what's wrong and help them get back on track.

Although the online learning space doesn't afford you the same level of constant, real-time feedback, you can get close by deliberately designing it into your course. Here's how.

Your Receptivity to Feedback

The first thing you need is an attitude of receptivity to feedback. As online course creators, we all need, want, and appreciate feedback in the form of testimonials and positive reviews. But there's a type of feedback you should be asking for from every learner, regarding every aspect of your course, from the very beginning, and that's direct feedback to you about what's working to help them learn the course material, and what's not. Keep asking at regular intervals until the end.

When launching a new course, you may get a lot of feedback at first about things that are not working as well as they could be. Your learners at this point have not had a chance to get the benefit of your expertise, but they can certainly notice (and may be annoyed) if a link is broken or a log-in doesn't work.

Hey, tech happens. The best thing you can do is be prepared for the inevitable glitches and provide a way for course participants to notify you the minute they experience one. Especially with a new course, your first participants are helping you find and fix anything that's not ideal, so ask for their input, be receptive to it, thank them profusely, and fix everything as soon as you possibly can.

Redundant Systems

If you can't fix something that your course depends on (for example, if your video-conferencing platform goes down for maintenance or your computer freezes up), you can save the day by having redundant systems in place. I learned about redundant systems when I worked in water, wastewater, and energy utilities. The services that utilities provide are so critical to the public communities they serve that failure is not an option, so utilities rely on redundant systems, which means having backup plans and extra equipment so that if any particular piece of machinery or part of a process is not working, there's always a workaround readily available.

What redundant systems mean for your online course is that you should have multiple ways to connect and communicate with your course participants and convey your course content to them. For example, if your video-conferencing platform experiences unexpected downtime, you could run your group meeting as a Facebook live, if need be. In a pinch, you could write up the week's lesson content in a Word doc and share the file with your students via Dropbox or email. This is another advantage to doing your instructional design first, before selecting your media and tech tools. If you're clear on what you need to teach at any particular time, you can find an alternate way to teach it if any particular piece of the technology pipeline is not working as planned.

Communication with your online course participants is another area where redundancy is needed. (By *redundancy,* I mean maintaining excess capacity and alternate methods that provide you with the ability to do the same thing in more than one way). For example, if you send an email to your course participants reminding them of the location for your live class meeting, it is also helpful to post the meeting link in your private Facebook group, in the course itself, and so on. You might need to post a meeting reminder a day or two in advance, on the day itself, and then again right before the meeting. You may also find that you need to repeat instructions and information that you've provided, more than once. Doing the same thing more than once, and in more than one way, may feel excessive or unnecessary to you as the course creator. That's because you are already an expert in the subject, you are the one sending the message, and you got it the first time. However, some of your course participants may not receive the email you sent, others may not check Facebook often or at all, some won't understand, and others may forget a reminder the first time they see it. As you gain experience running your course with your own students, both you and they will learn which communication channels work best to ensure that everyone receives, understands, and remembers your messages. Using multiple communication channels and backup methods will ensure everyone "gets the memo" in case your original, preferred method doesn't work.

Remember this underlying principle: just because you've said something (or written it) does not mean that the information has been taken in and processed by your course participants. There are so many things pulling on everyone's attention these days, that you need to be sure your message is getting through. (I'm not suggesting that we bombard our learners with too many emails. I'm saying check in with them and find out what channels and timeframes work best to communicate with them).

Teach People How to Provide Feedback

It's helpful to provide your learners with guidance on *how* to provide feedback to you and to each other, early in your course. Make sure they know that you want their feedback about what is and is not working for them in the course. Back that up by being receptive and responsive to the feedback they give. It's also helpful to provide guidance to the group as a whole, on how to provide feedback to each other in ways that are supportive while also pointing out what can be improved.

I learned the *sandwich technique* at Toastmasters (see "Resources") and find it to be useful. In this technique, you start by providing feedback about something positive you observed relative to the topic under discussion (that's the bottom piece of "bread" in the sandwich). Then you get to the "meat," which is your constructive feedback on what can be improved. And then you finish with another positive observation or encouragement for further improvement (the top slice of "bread").

Done right, the sandwich technique is an effective way to manage two important factors that must be in balance for learning to occur. On the one hand, learners must be able to maintain a sense of safety and self-esteem in order to be ready to learn anything new. (That includes you, as a course creator who is learning from your students about ways you can improve your course). The positive feedback (the "bread" in the sandwich) helps people feel ok about themselves and gives them the security to be ready to hear what they can do better. Learners do want to improve, and genuinely need to hear what they can do to achieve that. The constructive criticism (the "meat" in the sandwich) addresses that second factor by helping learners improve and grow.

Another reason to teach and use the sandwich technique is that it helps build community. People feel a sense of safety and community in a culture where they can count on others to recognize and appreciate the good things they've done, while also offering constructive feedback about what could be even better.

We've touched on the mindset needed to be open to learner feedback about your course. We've discussed the importance of promoting a positive climate for feedback to be given and received. But how do you actually make positive and supportive feedback happen?

One way is to include a survey with each large section (chapter or module) of your course. The survey does not have to be long and can function as a way for learners to give you feedback about how their learning process is unfolding. The method you choose to do this will depend on your course platform and the media choices it supports. Personally, I use Thinkific and find it helpful to create a multimedia lesson using a Google form, at the end of each section of my course. One reason I like Google forms is that you can set them up so that the learners receive an emailed copy of their responses. (See Appendix B, "Sample Survey," for an example of a survey you could use in a Google form at the end of a module in your course.)

You can include a similar but more global and comprehensive survey at the end of the whole course, requesting feedback on students' learning experience in the course as a whole.

The important point about requesting learner feedback is that you want to constantly be monitoring how your course design is working and how it is being received. You will see individual differences in how different people respond to the same material. Some of those differences are based on whether your learner takes a "right-brained" or "left-brained" approach, what their learning preferences are, and other individual factors. You can use this ongoing feedback to continually improve your course and make it more and more responsive to all of your learners' needs.

At the same time, it's important to realize that "done is better than perfect." Your course will never be perfect, because nothing is. Also, what is perfect for one learner might not work well for another. So be open to feedback, use it to continually improve your course as much as possible for all your learners, and then let it go, knowing you have done your very best.

The Course Design Formula®
Summary and Review

You'll be creating your learning content at various levels: the course level, the module level, the lesson level, and the learning object level.

Everything in your course must lead directly to the course learning goal. At each level, start by determining the learning goal for that level. Your course needs a single, clear learning goal, and so does each module, lesson, and learning object in your course. All of the smaller learning goals (at the module level and below) must lead to the learning goal for the course as a whole.

Design from the largest/highest level downward, in the following sequence:

1. Determine your course learning goal.
2. Discover the domain of learning for the course, based on its learning goal.
3. Set up your modules based on the course's domain of learning.
4. Set up the lessons inside each module.
5. Plan each lesson.
6. Select the media you will use to create each learning object within each lesson.
7. Build each lesson.

By starting at the highest, most inclusive level and working downward, you ensure that every item in your course contributes directly to helping your learners achieve the course learning goal, which is the transformation you are promising them. The learning goal for each component in your course must contribute to the larger learning goal of the course as a whole.

Structure each level of your course based on its learning goal. Use the course learning goal to determine which domain of learning your course, as a whole, falls into. This is the most important part of the whole process, because it determines the type of course structure you should use. Once you get this right (which can take some trial and error), everything else will fall into place.

Structure a **verbal information course** in chunks. Each module will provide one chunk of information, based on whatever chunking method you choose. Then divide each module into smaller chunks using either the same, or a different, chunking method for your lessons.

Set a **mindset course** up like this:
- Ineffective mindset choices
- The right (effective, helpful) mindset choice
- Role models

- Find your *why* (both your short-term and long-term motivations)
- Ongoing support

For a **cognitive strategy course** (learning how to learn about something), your modules will look like this.

- Explain the strategy
- Help learners practice the strategy
- Provide feedback

An **intellectual skills/ how to course** works best if set up like this.

- Big ideas
- Ingredients/tools
- Steps to perform the procedure
- Exceptions to the rules

If your course teaches **a motor skill (movement)** then set it up like this.

- Teach the individual movement components.
- Put the components together to create a movement routine.
- Help learners practice the routine.
- Provide immediate feedback.

- Provide ongoing practice (including mental rehearsal of the routine) until it's automatic.

Once you have your course structure set up, then structure each module based on its learning goal. For example, in a mindset course, the second module presents the effective mindset to adopt. Depending on what the effective mindset is, this module could be structured as verbal information, a cognitive strategy, a mindset within a mindset, an intellectual skill, or even a motor skill (for example, "Perform this yoga exercise every day").

Within each module, use Gagné's nine events of instruction to plan each lesson. Be sure to have a clear learning goal for each lesson (and be sure the lesson learning goal leads to the module learning goal, which in turn leads to the course learning goal).

When you present the instruction inside the lesson, be sure to present it according to the *lesson's* domain of learning. If your course is a mindset course, and Module 2 teaches a motor skill (how to do deep-breathing relaxation exercises before you get out of bed, for example), Lesson 1 of that module might teach verbal information that describes the various steps of the breathing exercise, while Lesson 2 takes the learner through actually performing the breathing exercise. Lesson 1 would be set up in small chunks of text or audio with relevant pictures (verbal information), and Lesson 2 would be set up to take learners through the actual breathing movements (motor skills).

By following these procedures at each level of your course, starting from the most comprehensive level and working your way down, you will ensure that everything in your course really needs to be there, is in the right place, and is helping your learners move closer to the course learning goal.

The purpose of assessment is to let you and your learners know if they've learned what they set out to learn. All assessments must refer back to the learning goal that is being assessed.

Scan your course outline and lesson plans to be sure everything is clear, engaging, and motivating.

Explore ways to include different learning modalities, multiple intelligences, and both lower- and higher-order thinking skills, in your course. Remember to use lower-order thinking skills in the beginning, when learners are just getting familiar with new concepts. Use higher-order thinking skills later in your course, to provide learners with opportunities to engage deeply with and use what they've learned.

By following the steps above, you will build the kind of structure and guidance into your course that helps learners overcome the cognitive load challenges posed by the online learning space.

You will create a course that is carefully structured to lead to the desired learning goal, in ways that guide your learners toward experiencing "light-bulb moments" for themselves.

You will also save yourself from getting stuck in the complexity and overwhelm many experts face when trying to figure out how to organize a lifetime's worth of wisdom into an effective online course.

Different Ways to Use the Course Design Formula®

You can use the formula at any stage of your course design process, from testing an idea for a pilot course, to revising and updating an existing one.

To quickly create a course mockup that you can test with your target audience, follow all the steps up to the part where you actually plan and build your lessons. You'll have a quick course prototype that makes it clear what benefits the course will deliver. Once you've tested the prototype with your target audience, you'll know whether to proceed with actually building out the course or modify it first and test again.

You can use the Course Design Formula® to:

- Test a variety of ideas to see which one to pilot.
- Run a pilot course.
- Build a full course after completing your pilot.
- Take an existing offline course and put it online.
- Revise and update an existing online course.

Once you learn this system you will be able to quickly and effectively structure any course, on any topic you want to teach. I'm thrilled and excited for you on your course creation journey. Keep me posted on how your course is coming along. I can't wait to see you create light-bulb moments for your course participants! Here's to your success . . . and theirs.

APPENDIX A

....

THE COURSE DESIGN FORMULA®
IN A NUTSHELL

To apply the formula to your course, follow these exact steps in this order:

1. Determine the one, all-encompassing transformation your course delivers.
2. Discover the course's domain of learning
3. Set up your modules based on the course's domain of learning.
4. Lay out the lessons inside each module based on the module's domain of learning.
5. Plan each lesson to include all nine of the nine events of instruction.
6. Select the optimal media to present each piece of content in each lesson.
7. Build your course.

As you go through those steps, remember the following principles.

- Every lesson must have a clear learning objective.
- The lesson learning objective must lead to the module learning objective.
- The module learning objective must lead to the course learning goal.
- Build guided practice, feedback, and assessment into every lesson.

APPENDIX B

....

SAMPLE SURVEY

Here are questions you could include in your survey:

- What worked well for you with this module, to help you learn (the module learning goal)?
- What could have worked better for you with this module?
- A few questions to help you find out the degree to which they've mastered the material in the module.
- A rating scale: how helpful was this module in helping you achieve the module learning goal?
- An open-ended question asking them to explain why they gave the module the rating they did.

Also leave a space for them to say anything else that they want to share about their experience with this module.

ACKNOWLEDGMENTS

If it takes a village to raise a child, it takes a city to raise a book—an international city that transcends space and time. This book is a love story, because real, deep teaching is an act of love. I want to express my profound love, thanks, and appreciation to everyone who made this book possible.

The first order of thanks goes to the people who contributed to materially producing the book: Thanks to Debbra Lupien for introducing me to my brilliant and insightful editor, Stephanie Gunning. Stephanie's gift for structure, detail, and marketing amaze me and have made this book all it can be. Huge thanks also to Gus Yoo for his magnificent cover design and to Najat Washington for so elegantly formatting the manuscript. A special debt of gratitude goes to the WebAIM team for their online training course for creating accessible documents, and to George Joeckel for his review of the information on accessibility issues in the manuscript. I also want to gratefully acknowledge my book launch team for all their hard work and support.

I am grateful to the following leaders in the world of digital marketing and online course development, who have inspired and supported my business development: Ryan Deiss and Russ Henneberry of Digital Marketer; Danny Iny, Lizzie Merritt, and Cheryl Woodhouse of Mirasee; Amy Porterfield and Marie Forleo, for their leadership and example as creative entrepreneurs; Chandler Bolt, Sean Sumner, R. E. Vance, Myles V. Holar, Emily Rose, and all my fellow writers at Self-Publishing School; Rob Balasabas, Aaron Morin, and the entire amazing tech support team at Thinkific.

A profound debt of gratitude goes out to my students in the pilot version of the Course Design Formula® Master Course. Thank you for being the first people on the planet to experience the Course Design Formula®, and for demonstrating its impact on your own courses. I am so thankful for you and so excited to see you become world-changing teachers in your respective areas of expertise.

To all of my coaching and consulting clients, whether we worked together for many sessions or just one, thank you for your dedication to creating powerful online learning and for demonstrating how the Course Design Formula® works for all kinds of subject matter.

I am thankful to all the schools and teachers that have nurtured me throughout the years from nursery school through graduate school and beyond: Miss Hazeltine's nursery school in Belmont, Massachusetts; the Town and Brearley Schools in New York City; Harvard University; Wheelock College Graduate School; Riverside Community College; Cerro Coso Community College; Pioneers Academy; the Qasid Institute, and California State University, San Bernardino. Special thanks to Suzie Ama, Elaine Jackson, Dr. Brian Newberry, Dr. Amy Leh, Dr. Eun-ok Baek, Dr. Dany Doueiri, Mauricio Cadavid, and Takiya Moore.

This book is a further elaboration of research that began with my master's training at California State University, San Bernardino. Dr. Brian Newberry, my master's project advisor, deserves the lion's share of credit for making this book possible. Thank you, Dr. Newberry, for forcing me to articulate what I was doing that made my classroom presentations work, and for helping me figure out how to turn that into something that would work equally well online. Thank you for your open mind and scientific inquiry, and for always being there to advise me while supervising probably one of the longest master's projects in history. I appreciate it more than I can say.

Personal mentors whose wisdom and guidance have shaped my life, teaching, and writing include Georgia Lambert Randall, Dr. Irvin Taube, Dr. Abraham Argun, and Kathleen Spivak. Thank you for inspiring me through your expertise, insight, and example.

I need to thank my friends and colleagues together in one group, because so many of my colleagues have become dear friends over the years. I have been so blessed to work with the most amazing professionals and wonderful human beings, whether teaching face to face or online. Your friendship and professionalism make work a joy. Profound thanks and appreciation go to my mentors, colleagues, and friends at Eastern Municipal Water District and Riverside Public Utilities, the education team at Metropolitan Water District, the entire Southern California water education community, and the hundreds of teachers and thousands of students who participated in my water and energy presentations over the years. To every teacher and every student who wrote me a personal letter after experiencing one of my presentations or field trips: thank you from the bottom of my heart. I read them all and appreciate your feedback more than I can say.

Special thanks to Jolene Allred Walsh, Mary Brown, Malea Ortloff, Steve Mains, Russ Donnelly, Dick Heil, Mike Bacich, Patty Estrada, Sarah Anne Tye, and all my student interns and helpers throughout the years.

Thanks to personal friends Rita and Harold Gutteriez and family, and Virginia and Vince Fesunoff and family, for your friendship, support, and encouragement over the years; and a special thank you to Virginia Fesunoff for the beautiful author photos for my website and book.

I want to express my deepest appreciation to my personal and professional support community, including Denise Williams, Albert Fanoga, John Huntley, Laura Gannon, Kathryn Goldman, Mark Ainley, Kim Stapleton, and Adam Frost. Thank you for your expertise and support that keeps my life and business healthy and organized and functioning optimally on all levels.

And finally, a profound debt of gratitude goes to my family for supporting and encouraging me throughout the long years it took for this book to come into existence.

John: Thank you for being my friend and traveling companion for the past thirty-five years, through marriage and parenthood to the steady flame of friendship built on years of shared experience. Thank you for all the healthy dinners cooked, the solid parenting shared, the wise advice you gave (whether I took it or not). Thank you for supporting me in having "a room of my own" while also providing the stability and warmth of family life. Thank you from the bottom of my heart for always being my rock.

Harry: Thank you for your warmth, your enthusiasm, your kindness, your flourless organic chocolate cake and homegrown vegetables, and your unflagging support of my work. Thank you for beta testing my courses and enthusiastically cheering my rough drafts. Thank you for believing in me, and for being one of my most enthusiastic supporters from day one.

Ben: Where can I begin? You were my first beta tester. The name of my business, Learn and Get Smarter, comes from what I used to say to you when I dropped you off at school every day. I am so proud to see that you have always taken those words to heart. You were and still are my reason for caring so deeply about passing on wisdom and tradition and knowledge and love. I am so proud of the person, artist, and teacher you have become. Teaching is the family business, and I see how you have absorbed it and made it your own, and now pass on your artistic vision to those who are eager to learn from you. I am so proud of you, Ben, and so honored and thankful that you are my son. You make it all worthwhile.

NOTES

Introduction

1. Instructional Design Central defines instructional design as the "process by which learning products and experiences are designed, developed, and delivered." See "Instructional Design Definitions: What Is Instructional Design," Instructional Design Central (accessed July 25, 2019), https://www.instructionaldesigncentral.com/what isinstructionaldesign.

2. C.M. Ho, M.E. Nelson, and W. Müeller-Wittig. "Design and Implementation of a Student-Generated Virtual Museum in a Language Curriculum to Enhance Collaborative Multimodal Meaning-Making," *Computers and Education,* vol. 57, no. 1 (2001), pp.1083–1097. Also see, Rebecca Frost Cuevas. "Turkish to Go: Teaching Intellectual Skills Online," *Electronic Theses, Projects, and Dissertations (accessed July 3, 2019),* p. 111, https://scholarworks.lib.csusb.edu/etd/111; and Richard E. Mayer and Roxana Moreno. "Nine Ways to Reduce Cognitive Load in Multimedia Learning," *Educational Psychologist,* vol. 38, no. 1 (2003), p. 48, doi:10.1207/S15326985EP3801_6.

3. Todd Tauber. "The Dirty Little Secret of Online Learning: Students Are Bored and Dropping Out," *Quartz* (March 21, 2013), https://qz.com/65408/the-dirty-little-secret-of-

online-learning-students-are-bored-and-dropping-out. Also see Owen Youngman and Quartz, "Thousands of People Sign Up for Online Classes They Never End Up Taking," *Quartz* (November 21, 2013), https://www.theatlantic.com/education/archive/2013/11/th ousands-of-people-sign-up-for-online-classes-they-never-end-up-taking/281709.

4. Sandra L. Colby and Jennifer M. Ortman. "The Baby Boom Cohort in the United States: 2012 to 2060. Current Population Reports," U.S. Census Bureau (May 2014), pp.1–16, https://www.census.gov/prod/2014pubs/ p25-1141.pdf.

5. Marc Prensky. "Digital Natives, Digital Immigrants," *On the Horizon,* vol. 9, no. 5 (October 2001), https://www.marcprensky.com/writing/Prensky%20-%20Digital%20Natives,%20Digital%20Immigrants%20-%20Part1.pdf.

6. Keith Krach. "Six Interesting Points on How 'Digital Natives' Think and Work," *Medium* (October 12, 2016), https://medium.com/@KeithKrach/6-interesting-points-on-how-digital-natives-think-and-work-4960cc3f6e8e.

7. Austin Gardner-Smith. "Meet Gen Z: The Social Generation," Hill Holliday, https://genz.hhcc.com/hubfs/ Gen%20Z%20-%20The%20Social%20Generation%20%7 C%20Hill%20Holliday-4.pdf?submissionGuid=e1937055-9a4a-400f-a5ab-f910a8b6fdbb. Also see, "Generation Z,"

Wikipedia (accessed July 3, 2019), https://en.wikipedia.org/wiki/Generation_Z.

8. Don Norman. *The Design of Everyday Things, Revised and Expanded Edition* (New York, N.Y.: Basic Books, 2013).

Chapter 1: What Is Learning?

1. Saul McLeod. *"Jean Piaget's Theory of Cognitive Development,"* Simply Psychology (June 6, 2018), https://www.simplypsychology.org/piaget.html.

2. "Working Memory," Wikipedia (accessed July 3, 2019), https://en.wikipedia.org/wiki/Working_memory.

3. George A. Miller. "The Magical Number Seven, Plus or Minus Two: Some Limits on Our Capacity for Processing Information," *Psychological Review,* vol. 101, no. 2 (1956), pp. 343–52, http://www2.psych.utoronto.ca/users/peterson/psy430s2001/Miller%20GA%20Magical%20Seven%20Psych%20Review%201955.pdf.

4. Susan C. Nurrenbern. "Piaget's Theory of Intellectual Development Revisited," *Journal of Chemical Education,* vol. 78, no. 8 (August 1, 2001), pp. 1107–10, https://pubs.acs.org/doi/10.1021/ed078p1107.1.

5. Paul Reber. "What Is the Memory Capacity?" *Scientific American* (May 1, 2010), https://www.scientificamerican.com/article/what-is-the-memory-capacity.

6. Rebecca Frost Cuevas. "Turkish Vowel Harmony," Turkish to Go (accessed April 9, 2014), pp. 34, 92, and 99, http://www.learnturkishtogo.com/course/view.php?id=5.

Also see: R.M. Gagné and M.P. Driscoll. *Essentials of Learning for Instruction, Second Edition* (Englewood Cliffs, N.J.: Prentice-Hall, 1988), p. 33; and K. Hasegawa, M. Ishikawa, N. Shinagawa, K. Kaneko, and H. Miyakoda. "Learning Effects of Self-made Vocabulary Learning Materials," *Proceedings of the IADIS International Conference on Cognition* (2008), p. 153.

7. Garson O'Toole "If I Had More Time, I Would Have Written a Shorter Letter," Quote Investigator (accessed July 3, 2019), https://quoteinvestigator.com/2012/04/28/shorter-letter.

8. Although there are some technical differences between them, I am using the terms *short-term memory* and *working memory* interchangeably in this book.

9. R.M. Gagné and M.P. Driscoll. *Essentials of Learning for Instruction, Second Edition* (Englewood Cliffs, N.J.: Prentice-Hall, 1988), p. v.

10. R.M. Gagné and M.P. Driscoll. *Essentials of Learning for Instruction, Second Edition* (Englewood Cliffs, N.J.: Prentice-Hall, 1988), pp. 31–5. Also see: K. Hasegawa, M. Ishikawa, N. Shinagawa, K. Kaneko, and H. Miyakoda. "Learning Effects of Self-made Vocabulary Learning Materials," *Proceedings of the IADIS International Conference on Cognition* (2008), p. 157.

11. John Sweller. "Cognitive Load During Problem Solving: Effects on Learning," *Cognitive Science*, vol. 12 (April 1988), pp. 257–85, doi:10.1207/s15516709cog1202_4.

12. J. van Merriënboer and P. Ayres. "Research on Cognitive Load Theory and Its Design Implications for e-Learning. *Educational Technology Research and Development,* vol. 53, no. 3 (2005), p. 5.

13. Fred Paas, Tamara van Gog, Optimising worked example instruction: Different ways to increase germane cognitive load, Learning and Instruction, vol. 16, no. 2 (2006), pp. 87–91, ISSN 0959-4752,

    https://doi.org/10.1016/j.learninstruc.2006.02.004. (http://www.sciencedirect.com/science/article/pii/S09594 75206000181).

14. Benjamin S. Bloom. *Taxonomy of Educational Objectives, Handbook I: The Cognitive Domain* (New York: David McKay, 1956).

15. Matthew Lynch. "How to Use Bloom's Digital Taxonomy," *Edvocate* (April 15, 2018), https://www.theed advocate.org/how-to-use-blooms-digital-taxonomy.

Chapter 4: How the Formula Works: An Overview

1. Great Schools Partnership. "Backward Design," Glossary of Education Reform (December 13, 2013), https://www.edglossary.org/backward-design. Also see: J. Schneider. "Backward Design," Learning Theories (accessed July 4, 2019), https://www.learning-theories.com/backward-design.html.

2. Stephen R. Covey. *The 7 Habits of Highly Effective People: Restoring the Character Ethic, Revised Edition* (New York: Free Press, 2004).

3. R.M. Gagné. "Domains of Learning," *Interchange,* vol.3, no. 1 (1972), pp. 1–8. Also: R.M. Gagné. *The Conditions of Learning and Theory of Instruction, Fourth Edition* (Orlando, FL.: Holt, Rinehart, and Winston, 1985); R.M. Gagné and L.J. Briggs. *Principles of Instructional Design* (New York: Holt, Rinehart, and Winston, 1974); R.M. Gagné and M.P. Driscoll. *Essentials of Learning for Instruction, Second Edition* (Englewood Cliffs, N.J.: Prentice-Hall, 1988); and R.M. Gagné, W.W. Wager, K.C. Golas, and J.M. Keller *Principles of Instructional Design, Fifth Edition* (Belmont, CA.: Wadsworth Cengage Learning, 2005).

4. R.M. Gagné. "Domains of Learning," *Interchange,* vol. 3, no. 1 (1972), pp. 1–8, http://dx.doi.org/10.1007/BF02145939.

5. Mike Sosteric and Susan Hesemeier. "When Is a Learning Object Not an Object: A First Step Towards a Theory of Learning Objects," *International Review of Research in Open and Distributed Learning,* vol. 3, no. 2 (2002). https://doi.org/10.19173/irrodl.v3i2.106. Also see: George M. Piskurich. *Rapid Instructional Design: Learning ID Fast and Right, Second Edition* (San Francisco, CA.: Pfeiffer, 2006), pp.299–300.

Chapter 6: Step 2: Discover the Specific Type of Learning Your Course Contains

1. R.M. Gagné. "Domains of Learning," *Interchange,* vol. 3, no. 1 (1972), pp. 1–8, http://dx.doi.org/10.1007/BF02145939.

2. Robert M. Gagne. "Learning Outcomes and Their Effects: Useful Categories of Human Performance," *American Psychologist* (April 1984),pp. 377–85, https://pdfs.semanticscholar.org/5306/72ba34ef7b284f5d6 235da825b3a1971a7fc.pdf.

3. R.M. Gagné and M.P. Driscoll. *Essentials of Learning for Instruction, Second Edition* (Englewood Cliffs, N.J.: Prentice-Hall, 1988), pp. 88–90.

4. Gagné. "Learning Outcomes and Their Effects." p. 381.

5. Gagné and Driscoll, pp. 95-97.

6. Ibid., p 96

7. R.M. Gagné, W.W. Wager, K.C. Golas, and J.M. Keller *Principles of Instructional Design, Fifth Edition* (Belmont, CA.: Wadsworth Cengage Learning, 2005), p. 94.

8. Ibid.

9. Gagne. "Learning Outcomes and Their Effects," p. 383.

10. Gagné, et al. *Principles of Instructional Design,* pp. 96–97.

11. Ibid., pp. 96–99.

12. Ibid., pp 98–99.

13. Ibid., p 99.

14. Ibid.

15. Ibid., p. 99.

16. Ibid.

17. Gagné and Driscoll, pp. 97–9, 115–16.

18. Gagné et al. *Principles of Instructional Design*, pp. 60–73.

19. Gagné and Driscoll, pp. 91–95.

20. Gagné et al. *Principles of Instructional Design*, p, 64.

21. Ibid, pp. 63–4. Also see: Gagné and Driscoll, pp. 48–9.

22. Gagné and Driscoll, pp. 49–51.

23. Gagné et al. *Principles of Instructional Design*, p. 69.

24. Ibid., p. 63

25. Ibid., pp. 67–8.

26. Ibid.

27. Ibid., pp. 100–2. Also see: Gagné and Driscoll, pp. 99–102.

28. Ibid.

29. R. M. Gagné and M.P. Driscoll. *Essentials of Learning for Instruction, Second Edition* (Englewood Cliffs, N.J.: Prentice-Hall, 1988), p. 101.

30. Coach's Eye Sports Video Analysis App, https://www.coachseye.com; and GoPro Stop Action Cameras and App, https://gopro.com/en/us.

31. Andrew Woodbury. "How VR Training Apps Are Finally Becoming a Reality," ReadWrite (March 30, 2017), http://readwrite.com/2017/03/30/how-vr-training-apps-are-finally-becoming-a-reality-ch; and: "Training Meets Virtual Reality: How to Create a Training App Using InstaVR," InstaVR (accessed July 5, 2019), https://www.instavr.co/articles/general/training-meets-virtual-reality-how-to-create-a-training-app-using-instavr.

32. John Ramsay. "Incorporating Virtual Reality (VR) into Online Courses," Imperial College London (July 15, 2016), http://wwwf.imperial.ac.uk/blog/ict-elearning/2016/07/15/incorporating-virtual-reality-vr-into-online-courses.

33. Gagné and Driscoll, p. 101.

34. Ibid.

35. L. Konge and L. Lonn. "Simulation-based Training of Surgical Skills," *Perspectives on Medical Education,* vol. 5, no. 1 (February 2016), pp. 3–4, https://www.ncbi.nlm.nih.gov/pmc/articles/PMC4754214. Also see: Richard L. Lammers, Moira Davenport, Frederick Korley, et al. "Teaching and Assessing Procedural Skills Using Simulation: Metrics and Methodology," *Academic Emergency Medicine,* vol. 15, no. 11 (November 3, 2008), pp. 1079–87, http://onlinelibrary.wiley.com/doi/10.1111/j.1553-2712.2008.00233.x/full.

Chapter 7: Step 3: Set Up Modules to Support Your Course's Learning Goal

1. R.M. Gagné, W.W. Wager, K.C. Golas, and J.M. Keller *Principles of Instructional Design, Fifth Edition* (Belmont, CA.: Wadsworth Cengage Learning, 2005), pp. 98–9. Also see: R. M. Gagné and M.P. Driscoll. *Essentials of Learning for Instruction, Second Edition* (Englewood Cliffs, N.J.: Prentice-Hall, 1988), pp. 97–9.

2. Ibid., p. 99.

3. Gagné et al. *Principles of Instructional Design*, pp. 67–8.

4. Ibid., pp. 100–2.

Chapter 8: Step 4: Plan and Set Up Your Lessons

1. R. M. Gagné and M.P. Driscoll. *Essentials of Learning for Instruction, Second Edition* (Englewood Cliffs, N.J.: Prentice-Hall, 1988), p. v.

2. R.M. Gagné, W.W. Wager, K.C. Golas, and J.M. Keller *Principles of Instructional Design, Fifth Edition* (Belmont, CA.: Wadsworth Cengage Learning, 2005), pp. 194–207.

3. S.D. Tripp and B. Bichelmeyer. "Rapid Prototyping: An Alternative Instructional Design Strategy," *Educational Technology Research and Development*, vol. 38, no. 1 (1990), pp. 31–44. Also see: G.M. Piskurich. *Rapid Instructional Design: Learning ID Fast and Right, Second Edition* (San Francisco, CA.: Pfeiffer, 2006), pp. 298–9.

4. Rebecca Frost Cuevas. "Turkish to Go: Teaching Intellectual Skills Online," Electronic Theses, Projects, and Dissertations (2014), p. 203, https://scholarworks.lib.csusb.edu/etd/111. Also see: W. Hung and R.J. McQueen. "Developing an Evaluation Instrument for e-Commerce Websites from the First-time Buyer's Viewpoint," *Electronic Journal of Information Systems Evaluation*, vol. 7, no. 1 (2004), p. 34.

5. Benjamin S. Bloom. *Taxonomy of Educational Objectives, Handbook I: The Cognitive Domain* (New York: David McKay, 1956).

6. Hoi K. Suen. "Peer Assessment for Massive Open Online Courses (MOOCs)," *International Review of Research in Open and Distributed Learning,* Athabasca University (July 2014), http://www.irrodl.org/index.php/ irrodl/article/view/1680/2904.

7. "Quick Quiz Guide," Moodle (accessed July 5, 2019), https://docs.moodle.org/37/en/Quiz_quick_guide.

8. Gagné et al. *Principles of Instructional Design,* pp. 201–2.

Chapter 9: Step 5: Select Your Media and Build Your Course

1. Richard E. Mayer. "Applying the Science of Learning: Evidence-based Principles for the Design of Multimedia Instruction," *American Psychologist,* vol. 63, no. 8 (2008), pp. 760–9.

2. Ibid., p. 761.

3. Ibid., p. 763.

4. Ibid., p. 762.

5. Ibid.

6. R.M. Gagné, W.W. Wager, K.C. Golas, and J.M. Keller *Principles of Instructional Design, Fifth Edition* (Belmont, CA.: Wadsworth Cengage Learning, 2005), pp. 201–2.

7. Mayer, pp. 760–9.

8. L.L. Lohr. *Creating Graphics for Learning and Performance: Lessons in Visual Literacy* (Upper Saddle River, N.J.: Pearson/Prentice-Hall, 2008). Also see: R.C. Clark and R.E. Mayer. *E-Learning and the Science of instruction: Proven*

Guidelines for Consumers and Designers of Multimedia Learning, Third Edition (San Francisco, CA.: Pfeiffer, 2011).

Chapter 11: Make Your Lessons Motivating

1. Stephen R. Covey. *The 7 Habits of Highly Effective People: Restoring the Character Ethic, Revised Edition* (New York: Free Press, 2004), p.160. Also see: Brett and Kate McKay. "The Eisenhower Decision Matrix: How to Distinguish Between Urgent and Important Tasks and Make Real Progress in Your Life," Art of Manliness (January 27, 2019), http://www.artofmanliness.com/2013/10/23/eisenhower-decision-matrix.

2. R. M. Gagné and M.P. Driscoll. *Essentials of Learning for Instruction, Second Edition* (Englewood Cliffs, N.J.: Prentice-Hall, 1988), pp. 64–6.

3. Ibid.

4. J.M. Keller. "Development and Use of the ARCS Model of Motivational Design," Association for Education and Training Technology (Exeter, England: 1983).

5. Gagné and Driscoll, pp. 71–80.

6. Rebecca Frost Cuevas. "Turkish to Go: Teaching Intellectual Skills Online," Electronic Theses, Projects, and Dissertations. (2014), pp. 32–3, https://scholarworks.lib. csusb.edu/etd/111.

7. Gagné and Driscoll, pp. 72–8. Also see: J.M. Keller, pp. 4–5; and Cuevas, pp. 109–10.

8. L.L. Lohr. *Creating Graphics for Learning and Performance: Lessons in Visual Literacy* (Upper Saddle River, N.J.: Pearson/Prentice-Hall, 2008), pp. 125–6. Also see: R. Mayer. "Applying the Science of Learning: Evidence-based Principles for the Design of Multimedia Instruction," *American Psychologist*, vol. 63, no. 8 (2008), p. 765; and R.C. Clark and R.E. Mayer. *E-Learning and the Science of Instruction: Proven Guidelines for Consumers and Designers of Multimedia Learning, Third Edition* (San Francisco, CA.: Pfeiffer, 2011), p. 238.

9. Gagné and Driscoll, pp, 134–7. Also see: K. Hasegawa, M. Ishikawa, N. Shinagawa, K. Kaneko, and H. Miyakoda. "Learning Effects of Self-made Vocabulary Learning Materials," *Proceedings of the IADIS International Conference on Cognition* (2008), p. 158; and Cuevas, p. 99.

Chapter 12: Make Your Learner the Focus as You Build Your Course

1. R. M. Gagné and M.P. Driscoll. *Essentials of Learning for Instruction, Second Edition* (Englewood Cliffs, N.J.: Prentice-Hall, 1988), pp. 85–91.

2. Rita Dunn, Jeffrey S. Beaudry, and Angela Klavas. "Survey of Research on Learning Styles," *California Journal of Science Education*, vol. 2, no. 2 (Spring 2002), p. 76, http://marric.us/files/CSTA_learnjournal.pdf#page=76. Also see: Yulong Li1, Jane Medwell, David Wray, Lixun Wang, and Xiaojing Liu. "Learning Styles: A Review of

Validity and Usefulness," *Journal of Education and Training Studies*, vol. 4, no. 10 (October 2016), pp. 90–4, https://files.eric.ed.gov/fulltext/EJ1111359.pdf.

3. Handout: "Learning Styles: The Four Modalities," Center for Student Learning at the Addlestone Library, College of Charleston (accessed July 6, 2019), http://csl.cofc.edu/documents/study-skills/online-library/learning_styles/learning_styles_the_four_modalities.pdf.

4. "Overview of Learning Styles," Learning-Styles-Online (accessed July 6, 2019), http://www.learning-styles-online.com/overview.

5. David Glenn. "Matching Teaching Style to Learning Style May Not Help Students," *Chronicle of Higher Education* (December 15, 2009), https://www.chronicle.com/article/Matching-Teaching-Style-to/49497.

6. Gagné and Driscoll, pp. 72–3. Also see: John M. Keller. "Development and use of the ARCS model of instructional design." *Journal of Instructional Development,* vol. 10, no. 3 (1987), p. 4. Also see: Rebecca Frost Cuevas. "Turkish to Go: Teaching Intellectual Skills Online," Electronic Theses, Projects, and Dissertations. (2014), p. 98, https://scholarworks.lib.csusb.edu/etd/111.

7. Landing page for the Zoom website: https://www.zoom.us.

8. C.M. Ho, M.E. Nelson, and W. Müeller-Wittig. "Design and Implementation of a Student-generated Virtual Museum in a Language Curriculum to Enhance Collaborative Multimodal Meaning-making," *Computers and Education*, vol. 57, no. 1 (2011), pp. 1083–97.

9. Marc T. Hamilton, Genevieve N. Healy, David W. Dunstan, Theodore W. Zderic, and Neville Owen. "Abstract: Too Little Exercise and Too Much Sitting: Inactivity Physiology and the Need for New Recommendations on Sedentary Behavior," *Current Cardiovascular Risk Reports*, vol. 2, no. 292 (July 2008), https://link.springer.com/article/10.1007/s12170-008-0054-8.

10. Howard Gardiner. *Frames of Mind: The Theory of Multiple Intelligences* (New York: Basic Books, 1983). Also see: "Resources," MI Oasis (accessed July 6, 2019), https://www.multipleintelligencesoasis.org/resources; and "Multiple Intelligences," American Institute for Learning and Human Development (accessed July 6, 2019), http://www.institute4learning.com/multiple_intelligences.php.

11. Jun-Ki Lee, Il-Sun Lee, and Yong-Ju Kwon. "Scan and Learn! Use of Quick Response Codes and Smartphones in a Biology Field Study," *American Biology Teacher*, vol. 73, no. 8 (October 2011), pp. 485–92.

12. Andrew Churches. "Bloom's Digital Taxonomy," University of Alabama at Birmingham (April 1, 2009), pp. 1–75,

https://www.uab.edu/elearning/images/facultytoolkit/blo
om_digital_taxonomy_v3_01web.pdf.

Chapter 13: Make Sure Your Course Is Working for All Your Learners

1. Press release: "Visual Impairment and Blindness Prevalence in the U.S. to Double by 2050 According to Study by USC Roski Eye Institute Researchers," University of Southern California Roski Eye Institute (May 16, 2016), http://eye.keckmedicine.org/?post_type=post_press_relea se&p=6541.

2. "Image ALT Tag Tips for HTML," Accessibility and Usability at Penn State (accessed July 6, 2019), http://accessibility.psu.edu/images/imageshtml.

3. "Designing for Screen Reader Compatibility," WebAIM (accessed July 6, 2019), https://webaim.org/techniques/ screenreader.

4. "Make Your Word Documents Accessible to People with Disabilities," Microsoft (accessed July 6, 2019), https://support.office.com/en-us/article/make-your-word-documents-accessible-to-people-with-disabilities-d9bf3683-87ac-47ea-b91a-78dcacb3c66d?ui=en-US&rs=en-US&ad=US. Also see: "Microsoft Word: Creating Accessible Documents," WebAIM (accessed July 6, 2019), http://webaim.org/techniques/word.

5. "Add Alternative Text to a Shape, Picture, Chart, SmartArt Graphic, or Other Object," Microsoft (accessed July 6, 2019), https://support.office.com/en-us/article/Add-alternative-text-to-a-shape-picture-chart-table-SmartArt-graphic-or-other-object-44989b2a-903c-4d9a-b742-6a75b451c669.

6. "Document Accessibility Course," WebAIM (accessed August 11, 2019), https://webaim.org/training/docs.

7. "Improve accessibility with the Accessibility Checker," Microsoft (accessed August 11, 2019), khttps://support.office.com/en-us/article/improve-accessibility-with-the-accessibility-checker-a16f6deo-2f39-4a2b-8bd8-5ad801426c7f.

8. "Create Accessible PDFs," Microsoft (accessed July 6, 1029), https://support.office.com/en-us/article/Create-accessible-PDFs-064625e0-56ea-4e16-ad71-3aa33bb4b7ed.

9. "Design Considerations: Text-only Versions," WebAIM (accessed July 6, 2019), http://webaim.org/articles/design/textonly.

10. Ruth C. Clark and Richard E. Mayer. *E-learning and the science of instruction: Proven guidelines for consumers and designers of multimedia learning, Third Edition* (San Francisco, CA.: Pfeiffer, 2011), p. 238.

Chapter 14: How to Adapt Face-to-Face Learning to Online (and How Not To)

1. Don Norman. *The Design of Everyday Things* (New York: Basic Books, 2002).

2. D. Allard, J. Bourdeau, and R. Mizoguchi. "Addressing Cultural and Native Language Interference in Second Language Acquisition," *CALICO Journal,* vol. 28, no. 3 (2011), pp. 677–98.

3. G.M. Piskurich. *Rapid Instructional Design: Learning ID Fast and Right, Second Edition* (San Francisco, CA.: Pfeiffer, 2006), pp. 16–19.

4. M. Nathan and A. Petrosino. "Expert Blind Spot among Preservice Teachers," *American Educational Research Journal,* vol. 40, no. 4 (2003), pp. 905–28.

5. Richard Mayer. "Applying the Science of Learning: Evidence-based Principles for the Design of Multimedia Instruction," *American Psychologist,* vol. 63, no. 8 (2008), pp. 760–9. Also see: Richard Clark and Ruth Mayer (2011). *e-Learning and the Science of Instruction: Proven Guidelines for Consumers and Designers of Multimedia Learning, Third Edition* (San Francisco, CA.: Pfeiffer, 2011), pp.72–4.

6. R.M. Gagné, W.W. Wager, K.C. Golas, and J.M. Keller *Principles of Instructional Design, Fifth Edition* (Belmont, CA.: Wadsworth Cengage Learning, 2005), pp. 64–73.

7. Cuevas, p. 203.

8. "Four Stages of Competence," Wikipedia (accessed July 6, 2019), https://en.wikipedia.org/wiki/Four_stages_of_competence.

9. Richard E. Mayer and Roxana Moreno. "Nine Ways to Reduce Cognitive Load in Multimedia Learning," *Educational Psychologist,* vol. 38, no. 1 (2003), p. 45, doi.org/10.1207/ S15326985EP3801_6.

Chapter 15: How to Create a Transformative Online Course

1. Jerome S. Bruner. (1961) "The Art of Discovery," *Harvard Educational Review,* vol. 31, no. 1 (1961), pp. 21–32.

2. Paul A. Kirschner, John Sweller, and Richard E. Clark (2006). "Why Minimal Guidance During Instruction Does Not Work: An Analysis of the Failure of Constructivist, Discovery, Problem-based, Experiential, and Inquiry-based Teaching," *Educational Psychologist,* vol. 41, no. 2 (2006), pp. 75–86. Also see: Richard E. Mayer. "Should There Be a Three-Strikes Rule Against Pure Discovery Learning?" *American Psychologist,* vol. 59, no. 1 (January 2004), pp. 14–9, https://psycnet.apa.org/doiLanding?doi=10.1037%2F0003-066X.59.1.14; and Juhani E. Tuovinen and John Sweller. "A Comparison of Cognitive Load Associated with Discovery Learning and Worked Examples," *Journal of Educational Psychology,* vol. 91, no. 2 (June 1999), pp. 334–341, https://psycnet.apa.org/doiLanding?doi=10.1037%2F0022-0663.91.2.334.

3. Ruth C. Clark and Richard E. Mayer (2011). *e-Learning and the Science of Instruction: Proven Guidelines for Consumers and Designers of Multimedia Learning, Third Edition* (San Francisco, CA.: Pfeiffer, 2011), p. 386. Also see: Kirschner, Sweller, and Clark, pp. 83–4; A.T. Stull and Ricahrd E. Mayer. "Learning by Doing Versus Learning by Viewing: Three Experimental Comparisons of Learner-generated Versus Author-provided Graphic Organizers," *Journal of Educational Psychology*, vol. 99, no. 4 (2007), pp. 808–20, doi:10.1037/0022-0663.99.4.808; and Rebecca Frost Cuevas. "Turkish to Go: Teaching Intellectual Skills Online," Electronic Theses, Projects, and Dissertations. (2014), pp. 20, 68, 245–6, https://scholarworks.lib.csusb.edu/etd/111.

4. Kirschner, Sweller, and Clark, p. 79.

5. Clark and Mayer, p. 20.

6. Richard E. Mayer and Roxana Moreno (2003) Nine Ways to Reduce Cognitive Load in Multimedia Learning, *Educational Psychologist,* vol. 38, no. 1, pp. 43–52, DOI: 10.1207/S15326985EP3801_6. Also see Clark and Mayer, p. 20.

7. Cuevas, p. 228.

BIBLIOGRAPHY

Allard, D., Bourdeau, J., and Mizoguchi, R. "Addressing cultural and native language interference in second language acquisition," *CALICO Journal*, vol. 28, no. 3 (2011), pp. 677–98.

Bruner, J. S.. *The Process of Education*. (Cambridge, MA.: Harvard University Press, 1960).

Bruner, J. S. *The Relevance of Education* (New York: W.W. Norton & Company, 1973).

Callison, D. Constructivism. *School Library Media Activities Monthly*, vol. 18, no. 4 (2001), p. 35.

Cassady, J. C. and Mullen, L. J. "Reconceptualizing electronic field trips: A Deweyian perspective," *Learning, Media and Technology*, vol. 31, no. 2 (2006), pp. 149–161. doi:10.1080/17439880600756720.

Clark, R. C. and Mayer, R. E. *e-Learning and the Science of Instruction: Proven Guidelines for Consumers and Designers of Multimedia, Third Edition* (Hoboken, N.J.: John Wiley, 2011).

Colblindor. *Coblis—Color Blindness Simulator* (accessed April 12, 2014), http://www.color-blindness.com/coblis-color-blindness-simulator.

Cordova, D. and Lepper, M. "Intrinsic motivation and the process of learning: Beneficial effects of contextualization, personalization, and choice," *Journal of Educational Psychology*, vol. 88, no. 4 (1996), pp. 715–30.

Covey, Stephen R. *The 7 Habits of Highly Effective People: Restoring the Character Ethic, Revised Edition* (New York: Free Press, 2004).

Cuevas, Rebecca Frost. *Annotated Bibliography for EDUC 601* (San Bernardino, CA.: personal communication, 2008).

Debue, Nicolas and van de Leemput, Cecile. "What does germane load mean? An empirical contribution to the cognitive load theory," *Frontiers in Psychology*, vol. 5 (2014), p. 1009, https://www.ncbi.nlm.nih.gov/pmc/articles/PMC4181236.

Gagné, R. M. "Domains of learning," *Interchange*, vol. 3, no. 1 (1972), pp. 1–8.

Gagné, R. M. *The Conditions of Learning and Theory of Instruction, Fourth Edition* (Orlando, FL.: Holt, Rinehart and Winston, 1985).

Gagné, R. M. and Briggs, L. J. *Principles of Instructional Design* (New York, N.Y.: Holt, Rinehart and Winston, 1974).

Gagné, R. M. and Driscoll, M. P. *Essentials of Learning for Instruction, Second Edition* (Englewood Cliffs, N.J.: Prentice-Hall, 1988).

Gagné, R. M., Wager, W. W., Golas, K. C., and Keller, J. M. *Principles of Instructional Design, Fifth Edition* (Belmont, CA.: Wadsworth Cengage Learning, 2005).

Hasegawa, K., Ishikawa, M., Shinagawa, N., Kaneko, K., and Miyakoda, H. "Learning effects of self-made vocabulary learning materials," *Proceedings of the IADIS International Conference on Cognition* (2008), p. 153.

Hmelo-Silver, C. "Problem-based learning: What and how do students learn?" *Educational Psychology Review*, vol. 16, no 3 (2004), pp. 235–66.

Ho, C. M., Nelson, M. E., and Müeller-Wittig, W. "Design and implementation of a student-generated virtual museum in a language curriculum to enhance collaborative multimodal meaning-making," *Computers & Education*, col. 57, no. 1 (2001), pp. 1083–97.

Hüllen, W. Robert M. "Gagné's prototypes of learning and foreign language teaching," *Glottodidactica*, vol. 11, no. 1 (1978), pp. 1–12.

Hung, W., and McQueen, R. J. "Developing an evaluation instrument for e-commerce web sites from the first time buyer's viewpoint," *Electronic Journal of Information Systems Evaluation*, vol. 7, no. 1 (2004), pp. 31–42.

Kabak, B., and Kazanina, N. "Listeners use vowel harmony and word-final stress to spot nonsense words: A study of Turkish and French," *Laboratory Phonology*, vol. 1, no. 1 (2010), pp. 207–24.

Keller, J. M. "Development and use of the ARCS model of motivational design." Paper presented at the annual meeting of the Association for Education and Training Technology in Exeter, England (1983).

Kirschner, P. "Cognitive load theory: Implications of cognitive load theory on the design of e-learning," *Learning and Instruction*, vol. 12 (2002), pp. 1–10.

Kirschner, P. A., Sweller, J., and Clark, R. E. "Why minimal guidance during instruction does not work: An analysis of the failure of constructivist, discovery, problem-based, experiential, and inquiry-based teaching," *Educational Psychologist*, vol. 41, no. 2 (2006), pp. 75–86.

Krug, Steve. *Rocket Surgery Made Easy: The Do-It-Yourself Guide to Finding and Fixing Usability Problems* (Berkeley, CA.: New Riders, 2010).

Lee, J. K., Lee, I. S., and Kwon, Y. J. "Scan and learn! Use of quick response codes and smartphones in a biology field study," *American Biology Teacher*, vol. 73, no. 8 (2011), pp. 485–92, doi:10.1525/abt.2011.73.8.11.

Lohr, Linda L. *Creating Graphics for Learning and Performance: Lessons in Visual Literacy, Second Edition* (Upper Saddle River, N.J.: Pearson/Prentice-Hall, 2008).

Masgoret, A. M., and Gardner, R. C. "Attitudes, motivation and second language learning: A meta-analysis of studies conducted by Gardner and Associates," *Language Learning*, vol. 53, no. 1 (March 2003), pp. 123–63.

Mayer, R. "Applying the science of learning: Evidence-based principles for the design of multimedia instruction," *American Psychologist*, vol. 63, no. 8 (2008), pp. 760–69.

Moodle Docs. "Coding," Moodle (retrieved May 12, 2014), http://docs.moodle.org/dev/Coding.

Moodle Docs. "Guest Role," Moodle (retrieved April 12, 2014), http://docs.moodle.org/24/en/Guest_role.

Moodle Docs. "Why can't people (guests) take a quiz without creating an account and logging in? FAQ #13," Moodle (retrieved April 9, 2014), http://docs.moodle.org/25/en/Quiz_FAQ#Why_can.27t_p eople_.28guests.29_take_a_quiz_without_creating_an_ac count_and_logging_in.3F.

Moreno, D., Hernández, A. A., Yang, M. C., et al. "Fundamental studies in design-by-analogy: A focus on domain-knowledge experts and applications to transactional design problems," *Design Studies*, vol. 35, no. 3 (2014), pp. 232–72, doi:10.1016/j.destud.2013.11.002.

Nathan, M., and Petrosino, A. "Expert blind spot among preservice teachers," *American Educational Research Journal*, vol. 40, no. 4 (2003), pp. 905–28.

Norman, Don A. *The Design of Everyday Things* (New York, N.Y.: Basic Books, 2002).

Nurrenbern, S. C. "Piaget's theory of intellectual development revisited," *Journal of Chemical Education*, vol. 78, no. 8 (2001), pp. 1107–10.

Piskurich, G. M. *Rapid Instructional Design: Learning ID Fast and Right, Second Edition* (San Francisco, CA.: Pfeiffer, 2006).

Raoofi, S., Chan, S., Mukundan, J., and Rashid, S. "Metacognition and second/foreign language learning," *English Language Teaching*, vol. 7, no. 1 (2014), p. 36, doi:10.5539/elt.v7n1p36.

Rast, R. "The use of prior linguistic knowledge in the early states of L3 acquisition," *International Review of Applied Linguistics in Language Teaching*, vol. 48, nos. 2–3 (2010), pp. 159–83, doi: 10.1515/iral.2010.008.

Reiser, R.A. and Dempsey, J.V. *Trends and Issues in Instructional Design and Technology, Fourth Edition* (New York: Pearson, 2017).

Rice, W. *Moodle E-Learning Course Development, Third Edition: A Complete Guide to Create and Develop Engaging e-Learning Courses with Moodle* (Birmingham, UK: PakT Publishing, 2015).

Rice, W. *Moodle Teaching Techniques: Creative Ways to Use Moodle for Constructing Online Learning Solutions* (Birmingham, UK: PakT Publishing, 2007).

Runco, M., and Nemiro, J. "Problem finding, creativity, and giftedness," *Roeper Review*, vol. 16, no. 4 (1994), pp. 235–41.

Sheard, J., and Markham, S. "Web-based learning environments: Developing a framework for evaluation," *Assessment and Evaluation in Higher Education*, vol. 30, no. 4 (2005), pp. 353–68.

Stowe, W. & Lin, L. "Rapid prototyping discussion board activities for an online environmental science course," in P. Resta, editor, *Proceedings of SITE 2012—Society for Information Technology and Teacher Education International Conference* (Austin, TX.: Association for the Advancement of Computing in Education, 2012), pp. 940–46, https://www.learntechlib.org/primary/p/39696.

Stull, A. T., and Mayer, R. E. "Learning by doing versus learning by viewing: Three experimental comparisons of learner-generated versus author-provided graphic organizers," *Journal of Educational Psychology*, vol. 99, no. 4 (2007), pp. 808–20, doi:10.1037/0022-0663.99.4.808.

Thomas, M., editor. *Handbook of Research on Web 2.0 and Second Language Learning* (Hershey, PA.: IGI Global, 2009).

Tripp, S. D., and Bichelmeyer, B. "Rapid prototyping: An alternative instructional design strategy," *Educational Technology Research and Development*, vol. 38, no. 1 (1990), pp. 31–44.

Van Merriënboer, J., and Ayres, P. "Research on cognitive load theory and its design implications for e-learning," *Educational Technology Research and Development*, vol. 53, no. 3 (2005), pp. 5–13.

Zlatev, J. "Situated embodied semantics and connectionist modeling," in J. Allenwood and P. Gardewnfors, editors. *Cognitive Semantics: Meaning and Cognition* (Amsterdam, NL.: John Benjamins, 1999), pp. 173–94.

ART CREDITS

Grateful acknowledgement is made for permission to reproduce images from the following sources.

Figure 7.4. Ruled paper: © pialhovik via iStock/Getty Images Plus. Faces: © youak via DigitalVision Vectors/Getty Images.

Figure 7.5.© Learn and Get Smarter, Inc.

Figure 7.6. Note paper: © Sezeryadigar via E+/Getty Images. Cutting board: © pepmiba via iStock/Getty Images Plus.

Figure 7.7.Note paper: © Sezeryadigar via E+/Getty Images. Man with weights: © MRBIG_PHOTOGRAPHY via E+/Getty Images.

Figure 8.1. House: © chuvipro via DigitalVision Vectors/Getty Images.

Figure 8.2. House: © chuvipro via DigitalVision Vectors/Getty Images.

Figure 8.3. House: © chuvipro via DigitalVision Vectors/Getty Images.

Figure 8.4. © RichVintage via E+/Getty Images.

Figure 8.5. © Learn and Get Smarter, Inc.

Figure 8.6. © Learn and Get Smarter, Inc.

Figure 9.1. House: © chuvipro via DigitalVision Vectors/Getty Images.

Figure 9.2. Inset art: © DrAfter123 via DigitalVision Vectors/Getty Images.

Figure 11.1. Hieroglyphic vase: © AlonzoDesign via DigitalVision Vectors/Getty Images. Traffic sign: © ChoochartSansong via iStock/Getty Images.

Figure 11.2. Climber: © SolStock via E+/Getty Images.

Figure 12.1.Icons: © Logorilla via DigitalVision Vectors/Getty Images.

NEXT STEPS

Now that you've learned how the Course Design Formula® works, here are some additional steps you can take that will help you use it to design your course.

CONNECT WITH ME

Learn and Get Smarter, Inc.
Website: www.learnandgetsmarter.com
Phone: +1 (951) 384-1461
Email: Rebecca@learnandgetsmarter.com

LinkedIn
Rebecca Frost Cuevas:
www.linkedin.com/in/rebeccafcuevas

Learn and Get Smarter, Inc.:
www.linkedin.com/company/learn-and-get-smarter-inc

Facebook
Course Design Formula® Community:
www.facebook.com/groups/coursedesignformula

YouTube
https://bit.ly/2kmjkvz

DOWNLOAD THE FREE RESOURCES MENTIONED IN THE BOOK

Come to www.learnandgetsmarter.com/FreeResources:

- Course Planning Journal
- Course Planning Course
- Domains of Learning Infographic
- Lesson Planning Template
- Course Learning Domain Quiz
- Rubric creation template
- Free Course Design Strategy Session
- Course Design Formula® Facebook Community

ENROLL IN A COURSE WITH ME

The Course Design Formula® Workbook
https://members.learnandgetsmarter.com/courses/the-course-design-formula-workbook

The Course Design Formula® Master Course
https://members.learnandgetsmarter.com/bundles/the-course-design-formula-master-course

JOIN COURSE CRAFTERS CAMP™, OUR PRIVATE MEMBERSHIP COMMUNITY

Graduates of the Course Design Formula® Master Course are eligible. For more information, write to Rebecca@learnandgetsmarter.com.

HIRE ME FOR COACHING

Book a "FREE strategy session" on my calendar to determine how I can best help you achieve your goals: https://go.oncehub.com/RebeccaCuevas

RETAIN ME FOR ONLINE LEARNING DESIGN GUIDANCE

Schedule a "FREE strategy session" on my calendar to discuss your personal or organizational needs: https://go.oncehub.com/RebeccaCuevas

RESOURCES

Here you can find many different resources mentioned throughout the book, as well as other tools related to the topics we've discussed. These will help you successfully implement what you've learned from reading the book and deepen your understanding of the principles we've been exploring together.

VIDEOS

Interview with Robert M. Gagné on "Making Learning More Effective & Efficient" (2:48)
https://www.youtube.com/watch?v=4hCp-c9GbHA

"Portrait of a Theorist—Robert Mills Gagné,"
Colorado State University Master's Program (10:34)
https://www.youtube.com/watch?v=FgDcUnObLqI

Common Sense Education,
"What Is Bloom's Digital Taxonomy?" (4:51)
https://www.youtube.com/watch?v=fqgTBwElPzU&ab_channel=CommonSenseEducation

TOOLS & APPS

The Coaches' Eye Video Coaching App
www.coachseye.com

Go Pro Video Camera
For motor skills training feedback and analysis.
https://gopro.com/en/us

Quizlet
For teaching vocabulary and memorization.
https://quizlet.com

VoiceThread Cloud-based App
For creating asynchronous conversations.
https://voicethread.com

Flipsnack
For turning your PDFs into digital flipbooks.
www.flipsnack.com

TRAINING ORGANIZATIONS

WebAIM
Offers web accessibility training.
https://webaim.org

Toastmasters International
Offers public speaking training.
www.toastmasters.org

DIGITAL IMAGE LIBRARIES

Check the license of *every* image you want to use to ensure you are legally allowed to use it for your intended purpose.

Pixabay
https://pixabay.com

Unsplash
https://unsplash.com

Pexels
https://www.pexels.com

iStock Photo
www.istockphoto.com

Getty Images
www.gettyimages.com

TOOLS FOR ACCESSIBILITY

Accessibility is a complex issue. This list is provided as a convenience to help course designers start to focus on making their course materials accessible. However, it is not a complete or comprehensive list of all accessibility resources and is not to be relied on as such. The author (Rebecca Frost Cuevas) and publisher (Learn and Get Smarter, Inc.) make no warranties or guarantees about anything on or off this list.

World Wide Web Consortium (W3C®)
Accessibility Initiative

Home:
https://www.w3.org/WAI

Fundamentals:
https://www.w3.org/WAI/fundamentals/
accessibility-intro

Test and Evaluate:
https://www.w3.org/WAI/test-evaluate

Easy Check Page Review:
https://www.w3.org/WAI/test-evaluate/preliminary

Tools:
https://www.w3.org/WAI/ER/tools

WebAIM
Evaluation Tool:
https://wave.webaim.org

Accessible Documents Course:
https://webaim.learn.usu.edu

Color Contrast Checker:
https://webaim.org/resources/contrastchecker

Guide to PDF Accessibility:
https://webaim.org/techniques/acrobat/acrobat

California Department of Rehabilitation
www.dor.ca.gov/Home/AB434

Government-wide IT Accessibility Program
Guidance on creating accessible documents in MS
Word. https://section508.gov/create/documents

Microsoft Support
Search for the term "create accessible documents" at:
https://support.office.com

Colblindor Color Blindness Simulator
https://www.color-blindness.com/coblis-color-blindness-simulator

LEARNING STYLES & MULTIPLE INTELLIGENCES

Learning Styles Online
https://www.learning-styles-online.com

American Institute for Learning and Human Development
https://www.institute4learning.com/resources/articles/multiple-intelligences

Center for Teaching and Learning
https://ctl.learninghouse.com/kinesthetic-learning-online-learning-environment

E-Learning Industry
https://elearningindustry.com/multiple-intelligences-in-elearning-the-theory-and-its-impact

Department of Educational Psychology and Instructional Technology, University of Georgia
http://epltt.coe.uga.edu/index.php?title=Multiple_Intelligences_and_Learning_Styles

Bloom's Taxonomy, Andrew Churches
http://burtonslifelearning.pbworks.com/f/
BloomDigitalTaxonomy2001.pdf

TOOLS FOR CREATING RUBRICS

"How to Create a Rubric in Six Steps," ThoughtCo.
https://www.thoughtco.com/how-to-
create-a-rubric-4061367

"Rubric Maker," PBIS Rewards
Find links here to rubric-creation tools.
https://www.pbisrewards.com/blog/
free-online-rubric-maker

"Evaluation Rubrics a Valuable Tool for Assessing
eLearning," Learning Solutions
https://learningsolutionsmag.com/articles/evaluation-
rubrics-a-valuable-tool-for-assessing-elearning

ABOUT THE AUTHOR

Rebecca Frost Cuevas, founder and CEO of Learn and Get Smarter, Inc., is a leading online learning education consultant and trainer for experts and entrepreneurs. She holds a bachelor's degree in English from Harvard University, as well as two master's degrees in education. Her first master's, from Wheelock College Graduate School, is in curriculum design and development. Her second, from California State University, San Bernardino, is in instructional technology.

For fifteen years, Rebecca designed and delivered award-winning education programs for public utilities in Southern California, impacting over 150,000 students with hands-on learning experiences relating to water and energy conservation. The education programs she created won national and regional awards, including the prestigious Community Service Award from the American Public Power Association and the prominent Clair A. Hill Award from the Association of California Water Agencies. Rebecca also received multiple federal scholarships for international study, and (fun fact!) learned Photoshop and Illustrator at a technical school in a foreign language, where she was the only nonnative speaker in the class. She brings a creative, multicultural perspective to her work in educational consulting, instructional design, and curriculum development.

When not designing online courses, Rebecca enjoys making up stories about Mother Rebecca, a 200-year-old fictional Victorian know-it-all, who provides gracious solutions to life's perplexing problems. Back in the twenty-first century, Rebecca is the proud mother of an internationally known fiber artist who is famous for having knitted a life-sized human skeleton. She enjoys living in sunny southern California while staying in touch with friends from all over the world—and is proud to say that her sticky date pudding once took third prize at the National Date Festival.

Learn about Rebecca's products and services at www.learnandgetsmarter.com or contact her directly at Rebecca@learnandgetsmarter.com.

WRITE TO ME

How has your experience been using the methods described here? I'd love to hear from you with your thoughts and questions about *The Course Design Formula*®. Email me at Rebecca@learnandgetsmarter.com.

Made in the USA
Coppell, TX
01 January 2024

27110232R00246